Doctoral Proposal Writing

Doctoral Proposal Writing is an essential guide for current and prospective international doctoral students wishing to apply and study for a PhD in the UK, and other countries where courses are conducted in English.

The book supports students in choosing a suitable research topic and writing an effective proposal for investigating this topic across a range of forms of doctoral research, across several disciplines, with an emphasis on international students and students with English as an additional language. The author offers guidance for prospective doctoral students in their applications to study for a doctorate, in writing their initial proposals once they have been enrolled and, if necessary, in writing subsequent extended proposals. The book also includes content on developing academic writing, including paragraph writing, argumentation, doing literature reviews, constructing methodologies and using evidence and referencing. The book ends by covering giving a proposal presentation, how to get the most out of supervisory relationships and thinking about the next steps in your research.

By giving insights into the doctoral journey, and using real-life examples of good-quality doctoral proposals by international students, this is an essential resource for anyone looking to study for a PhD in the UK or anglophone countries.

Peter Samuels is a Senior Lecturer in Research Practice in the Graduate School of Management at Birmingham City University, UK. He has a background in education research, academic writing training and applied statistics support. He lectures in proposal writing and research methods and coordinates the supervision of about 1,500 masters research projects per year.

"This book provides over and above that to avail important tips about academic writing, defending the proposal, research management and managing relationships. It is a book about research proposal writing, but beyond that a manual for acquiring valuable research skills for application beyond the development process and defence of a doctoral proposal.

The international students' community and their supporters will find this book an important resource in the researcher development process."

Dr Loice Natukunda, *Lecturer in Research Methods,*
Lincoln International Business School, UK

"It will be clear to anyone reading this book that Peter's awareness of the challenges for students, especially international students, undertaking doctoral work is very informed by his career experiences and his book is carefully written to be as concise, clear, helpful, and user-friendly as possible to its potential audience.

In sum, if you are an international doctoral candidate who wants to write a solid proposal and, in the process, greatly increase your chances of being accepted onto a doctoral programme, you would be very well advised to read and digest Peter's book!"

Dr Andrew Hambler, *Associate Professor,*
Human Resource Management and Employment Law,
Birmingham City Business School, UK

Doctoral Proposal Writing
A Guide for International Students

Peter Samuels

LONDON AND NEW YORK

Designed cover image: cweimer4 / Getty Images

First published 2025
by Routledge
4 Park Square, Milton Park, Abingdon, Oxon OX14 4RN

and by Routledge
605 Third Avenue, New York, NY 10158

Routledge is an imprint of the Taylor & Francis Group, an informa business

© 2025 Peter Samuels

The right of Peter Samuels to be identified as author of this work has been asserted in accordance with sections 77 and 78 of the Copyright, Designs and Patents Act 1988.

All rights reserved. No part of this book may be reprinted or reproduced or utilised in any form or by any electronic, mechanical, or other means, now known or hereafter invented, including photocopying and recording, or in any information storage or retrieval system, without permission in writing from the publishers.

Trademark notice: Product or corporate names may be trademarks or registered trademarks, and are used only for identification and explanation without intent to infringe.

British Library Cataloguing-in-Publication Data
A catalogue record for this book is available from the British Library

ISBN: 978-1-032-56192-9 (hbk)
ISBN: 978-1-032-56193-6 (pbk)
ISBN: 978-1-003-43434-4 (ebk)

DOI: 10.4324/9781003434344

Typeset in Optima
by KnowledgeWorks Global Ltd.

Contents

Preface xi

Why this book? xi
Why the bear and the fish? xi
What is unique about this book? xi
Who is the author? xii
Acknowledgements xii
Reference xii

Foreword xiii

DR LOICE NATUKUNDA XIII
DR ANDREW HAMBLER XIV

PART I
Introducing the doctoral proposal 1

Introduction 3

Context 3
What is a proposal? 3
Why write a proposal? 3
What makes a good proposal? 3
Added benefits 4
Types of doctoral thesis 4
Outline of the rest of this book 4
References 6

1 The doctoral journey 7

The doctoral opportunity and challenge 7
Phases of a research project 7
Benefits of undertaking a doctorate 8
Reference 8

PART II
Selecting and presenting your topic — 9

2 Selecting your topic — 11

Introduction 11
The creative process 11
The importance of data 13
Other topic selection strategies 14
Qualities of a good topic 14
Exercise 15
Summary 15
References 15

3 Writing your front matter — 16

Introduction 16
Writing your title 16
Writing your aim 18
Writing your objectives 18
Writing your research questions 19
Exercises 20
Summary 20

PART III
Academic writing — 21

4 Structuring your proposal — 23

Introduction 23
Essential and optional elements of a proposal 23
Using section numbering 24
Summary 26
Reference 26

5 Academic writing style — 27

Introduction: busting a common myth 27
Use the third person, passive voice 27
Some dos and don'ts 28
Avoiding subjective writing 30
Use hedging 31
Summary 32
Reference 32

6 Using evidence — 33

Introduction 33
Backing up specific claims 33

Avoiding plagiarism and AI generation 34
Quoting 34
Summarising 35
Summary 36
References 36

7 Paragraph writing   37

Introduction 37
Definition 37
Length 37
Structure 37
Using transitional words 38
Examples 39
Summary 40
Reference 40

8 Argumentation   41

Introduction 41
Two styles 41
Examples 42
Argument planning 43
Example 44
Exercise 44
Summary 45
Reference 45

PART IV
Writing the rest of your proposal   47

9 Writing the rest of your introduction   49

Introduction 49
Writing your background 49
Example 49
Writing your problem statement 50
Example 50
Additional parts 51
Examples 51
Summary 53

10 Literature reviews   54

Introduction 54
General principles 55
Obtaining evidence 55
Deciding on your themes 57

viii *Contents*

    Including theory 57
    Including critical analysis 59
    Concluding your review 61
    Exercise 61
    Summary 62
    References 62

11 Conceptual frameworks   63

    Introduction 63
    Examples 63
    Exercise 64
    Summary 65
    References 65

12 Writing your methodology/method section   66

    Introduction: why the name confusion? 66
    Purpose and argumentation style 67
    Structure 67
    Philosophy 68
    Approach 69
    Strategy 70
    Data collection 72
    Validity, reliability and hypotheses 73
    Data analysis 74
    Ethics 76
    Limitations 77
    Common mistakes 77
    Evaluating methodology/methods sections: DECJAD 78
    Exercise 79
    Summary 79
    References 79

13 Producing a schedule and a budget   81

    Gantt charts 81
    Research phases 81
    Accompanying narrative 83
    Providing a budget 83
    Exercise 84
    Summary 84
    Reference 85

14 Referencing   86

    Introduction 86
    Citing 86

Tables and figures 88
Reference lists 89
Summary 91
References 92

PART V
After submitting your proposal 93

Introduction 93

15 Presenting and defending your proposal 95

Introduction 95
Developing a proposal presentation 95
Recommended structure 97
Delivering your presentation 98
Handling questions after your presentation 99
Summary 99
References 99

16 Writing another proposal 100

Introduction 100
Addressing feedback on your proposal 100
Understanding the requirements for another proposal 101
Turning your initial proposal into an extended one 102
Summary 102

17 Planning and managing your research 103

Time management 103
Stress management 106
Summary 107
References 108

18 Managing your supervisory relationships 109

Introduction 109
Models of supervision 109
Having appropriate expectations 111
Preparing for supervisions 112
Learning to be assertive 113
Additional advice for successful supervisory relationships 114
Summary 116
References 116

19 Next steps in your research 117

Introduction 117
Drafting your introduction chapter 117
Doing and drafting your full literature review 117
Drafting your methodology/methods chapter 118
Requesting ethics approval 118
Designing your data collection instrument 119
Summary 119
Bibliography 119

Index 121

Preface

Why this book?

Hello. My name is Dr Peter Samuels and I work for Birmingham City University. This is my second book Taylor and Francis have agreed to publish. My first book was on *Proposal Writing for Business Research Projects* at the undergraduate and master's levels (Samuels, 2023). However, my real passion is to train international doctoral students in proposal writing in any discipline, so the publishers kindly agreed to allow me to write this follow-up book using a similar style.

This book is targeted at doctoral students starting to undertake their research projects in English. It is assumed that the reader is either an international student who has travelled to an English-speaking country or is studying in their home country where English is an international language. In the rest of this book, I address you in the second person based on these assumptions.

Unlike my first book, this book is aimed at all disciplines, but there is an emphasis on **social science**. It is aimed at professional doctorates as well as traditional PhDs. This is due to my experience in my current job and also in my voluntary work.

Why the bear and the fish?

The picture of the bear eating fish on the cover represents the main message of this book: the importance of **putting the reader first**.

Bears are omnivores: part of the year they hibernate because there is not enough food. Sometimes they need to strategize because have too much food, such as when there are too many fish. A bear represents your **target reader** (who, like a bear in the fish spawning season, is probably very busy). Your proposal is the fish. Your target reader will have a strategy of which parts of your proposal to read first and what to expect from them. By following the principles explained in this book, you will be able to give them a good taste.

What is unique about this book?

This book uses actual examples of writing from international doctoral students. It also emphasises academic writing development within the proposal writing process. This is often a challenge for international students whose first language may not be English or who may have a non-literary background.

The final part of this book addresses the next steps in your doctoral journey after you submit your proposal.

Who is the author?

I am a Senior Lecturer in Research Practice at the Graduate School of Management at Birmingham City University. I have been teaching dissertation writing for over 13 years. I am currently responsible for teaching and coordinating the supervision of over 1,500 master's research project students every year. I am also the Course Director for our Doctor of Business Administration programme. I am also involved in voluntary work in East Africa where I provide intensive training courses on proposal writing to doctoral students in many different disciplinary areas.

Acknowledgements

I would sincerely like to thank five doctoral students who allowed me to use their proposals as examples in this book. Their first names are David, Dominique, Esther, Hashituky and Lee. Each of them wrote their proposal to a good standard, but they were not perfect. They therefore provide useful examples for learning purposes. They are mainly from East Africa whilst one is from the UK. They cover the academic disciplines of business administration, data science, design, mathematics education and science education. Four are from PhD studies whilst one is from a professional doctorate.

I would also like to thank my colleague Andrew Hambler for being my critical friend in the writing of this book. I acknowledge the assistance of Serve and Thrive Academy (https://serve-and-thrive-academy.thinkific.com, serveandthrive22@gmail.com) in the proof reading of this book.

Reference

Samuels, P. C. (2023). *Proposal Writing for Business Research Projects*. London: Taylor and Francis.

Foreword

Dr Loice Natukunda

Doctoral research can be one of the most challenging and yet very rewarding independent projects one undertakes in their career journey. It stretches cognitive ability, imagination, and creativity to design, execute and communicate an inquiry in a convincing and exciting manner. But once it is done, it can bring lasting satisfaction and be a source of much needed confidence in the pursuit of one's vision for their life.

Writing the doctoral research proposal provides the student with an opportunity to express intellectual and practical puzzles they are motivated about, suggest preferred methodological approaches to exploring those problems and receive input from various players in the process of shaping their ideas. The process is preceded by a decision to embark on a doctoral journey, where to enrol for a PhD and who to work with. Dr Samuels has thoughtfully brought to the attention of the users of this book the importance of reflecting on the opportunities and challenges along the doctoral journey. This is a generous mention in a book about doctoral proposal writing.

One of the challenges I encountered as an international doctoral student was the level of independence my supervisors expected me to have. Autonomy in decision-making concerning, especially, the process of shaping the focus of my study was daunting. I was, as Peter stated, "used to being told what to do". Peter correctly noted in this book that many students find divergent thinking disturbing and yet it is part of creative thinking through which a research topic is identified and shaped. Based on good examples, this book provides students from an educational background as mine valuable information on how to base their topic selection on existent credible data and creatively shape and validate their ideas.

Getting detailed guidelines about contents of a good proposal and how to write each aspect of it is hugely resourceful for international students juggling the language barrier and universal standards for proposal writing that clash with their cultural background. It is refreshing to find in one book these guidelines with relevant examples and exercises to try out. This book provides over and above that to avail important tips about academic writing, defending the proposal, research management and managing relationships. It is a book about research proposal writing, but beyond that a manual for acquiring valuable research skills for application beyond the development process and defence of a doctoral proposal.

I have sat under the tutelage of Dr Peter Samuels on many occasions during his virtual and in-person research capacity building visits to Uganda. He demystifies complexities about various aspects of research and the research journey. I am pleased that his wisdom and passion for international students and early career researchers have been consolidated in a book for an audience wider than would otherwise be possible for him to reach directly. The international students' community and their supporters will find this book an important resource in the researcher development process.

Thank you, Peter, for your sacrifices and the lasting contribution to international researcher development initiatives. May this book impact many on their research journey.

Dr Loice Natukunda
Lecturer in Research Methods
Lincoln International Business School

Dr Andrew Hambler

It is a particular pleasure to write this forward for a timely and extremely practical book on writing doctoral research proposals. The author, Dr Peter Samuels (a close colleague of mine for many years), has identified a real gap in the literature (in the same way as all good doctoral students should also do)! Whereas there is a welter of helpful textbooks concerning research methods in toto, as Peter has recognised, there is a real dearth when it comes to the vital business of proposal writing.

Why is this vital? Simply that potential doctoral candidates who produce proposals with gaps or areas of weakness are likely to be overlooked, or worse, actively avoided, by busy academics who want to engage with PhD, or professional doctoral, students who they consider are ready to start their doctoral journey, having adequately conceptualised a topic and identified a credible approach to undertaking research in that area. Few experienced supervisors want to work with doctoral students they fear will be poorly prepared and a drain on time and resources. Doctoral candidates therefore need to craft their proposals with great care in order to maximise their chances of being accepted and Peter's book provides comprehensive insights to help them to do so.

As a result of this second book, Peter has cemented his reputation as the key writer in the field of research project proposal writing and extended his repertoire to the group he has a particular passion for – international students who are interested in undertaking doctoral work. Peter is very experienced indeed in working with doctoral students in these very circumstances, either within the United Kingdom or elsewhere in the world – not least in Africa, where he has built up extensive networks.

Although Peter began his career as a Cambridge-educated mathematician, he has also worked in the past as an academic writing specialist and tutor – and I think it will be clear to anyone reading this book that Peter's awareness of the challenges for students, especially international students, undertaking doctoral work is very informed by his career experiences and his book is carefully written to be as concise, clear, helpful, and user-friendly as possible to its potential audience.

In sum, if you are an international doctoral candidate who wants to write a solid proposal and, in the process, greatly increase your chances of being accepted onto a doctoral programme, you would be very well advised to read and digest Peter's book!

Dr Andrew Hamber
Associate Professor, Human Resource
Management and Employment Law
Birmingham City Business School

Part I
Introducing the doctoral proposal

Introduction

Context

This book assumes that you are undertaking, or considering whether to undertake, a doctoral degree in English in any academic subject.

What is a proposal?

A proposal is a **structured document setting out what a researcher intends to do** in a research study. It usually contains a title, an introduction, a literature review, a method/methodological section and a schedule of events.

Why write a proposal?

Doctoral students are usually required to write one or more proposals for their intended research projects. These vary in length from a brief **concept note** at the stage of applying for a place on a doctoral programme to an **extended proposal** after a significant period of enrolment, which may be equivalent to the first three chapters of their final thesis.

The main purpose of a proposal is to persuade the academic staff responsible for reviewing proposals that you have chosen a viable research project in a context which you understand and that you have a credible plan to carry it out.

As proposal reviewers are busy people, **they will not be impressed by long words, complex sentences, irrelevant information or complex ideas**. Instead, they are looking for relevant clear ideas combined in a simple way. They will be persuaded by a **clear and concise argument** that is correctly structured and written.

What makes a good proposal?

The first and most important aspect of a good proposal is to **choose a good topic**. This means that it should be **within the scope of the doctoral programme**, of **interest** and **importance** to some relevant academic or social community and **narrowly focused** so that it is **original** and **achievable**.

Secondly, your argument for choosing your topic (known as your **rationale**) needs to be **clear** and **persuasive**.

Thirdly, you need to demonstrate that you **understand the context** of your chosen topic in your background and literature review.

Fourthly, you need to have a **credible and persuasive plan** for collecting and analysing your data (your **method**), the theoretical context of this plan (your **methodology**) and its practical outworking over the time and resources available (your **schedule** and **budget**).

Finally, your proposal needs to be well written and presented and follow the correct academic writing conventions.

Added benefits

Proposal writing is aligned with the first phase of the doctoral journey and is often the first subject for discussion with your new supervisory team. It therefore acts as a **gateway** into your doctoral research experience.

Learning how to write a good proposal can help you to become a better academic writer. As I have seen this working in practice I have chosen to do voluntary work, helping doctoral students in other countries understand these principles.

Types of doctoral thesis

All doctoral theses involve the **systematic collection and analysis of data**. However, in some places in this book, it is important to understand the difference between the two main types of thesis:

1 A **primary research thesis** involves the researcher **collecting and analysing some data themselves**, for example, by carrying out a questionnaire or interview.
2 A **secondary data thesis** involves the researcher **analysing a data set that someone else has already collected**. For example, this could be data on the financial performance of organisations, or some form of textual data already available in the public domain, such as customer comments on a product, or advertising on social media or company reports. However, this does not include published journal articles, as these are generally only reviewed in a thesis literature review.

Both these kinds of thesis involve carrying out a literature review before the data is collected and analysed. This kind of review may be undertaken using either a **narrative** or a **systematic** method. For an introduction to systematic reviews, please refer to Hemingway and Brereton (2009).

It is also useful at this stage to explain three general terms relating to **types of research**:

- **Quantitative research** refers to the analysis of **measurable quantities**, such as numbers and frequencies, which may involve decision-making about specific claims, known as **hypotheses**.
- **Qualitative research** refers to the analysis and interpretation of rich data collected from social settings, often in **textual** form.
- **Mixed methods research** refers to a combination of qualitative and quantitative research.

Outline of the rest of this book

The rest of Part I is a chapter on the doctoral journey.
The rest of this book is divided into four more parts.

Part II: selecting and presenting your topic

This part covers the topic selection and presentation process. Chapter 2 is about how to select your topic, whilst Chapter 3 explains how to present your chosen topic with what I call its **front matter**.

Part III: academic writing

The third part covers some of the principles of academic writing. The different competences involved in academic writing can be viewed as a tree, as shown in Figure 0.1.

The competencies below the dotted line have to do with writing general English rather than academic English (known as **functional skills**). For more information on these, please refer to Bailey (2018) and Gillett (2021). All the other competences are covered in this part except for document genre (as proposals are a type of document genre).

Chapter 4 explains how to structure your proposal. Chapter 5 introduces basic aspects of academic writing style. Chapter 6 covers issues of academic integrity, including the correct use of evidence and avoiding plagiarism, including the misuse of artificial intelligence (AI). Chapter 7 explains the principles of paragraph writing. Finally, Chapter 8 introduces the two main argumentation styles and how to plan your argument.

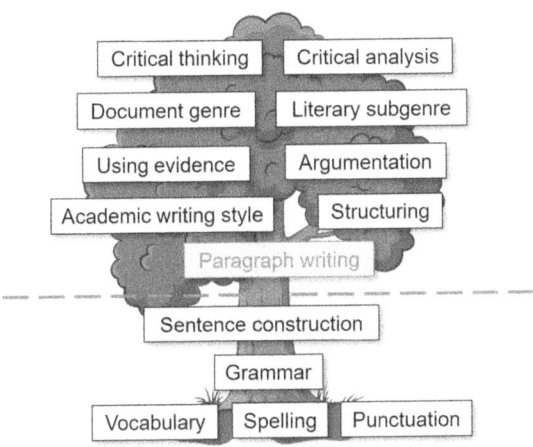

Figure 0.1 The academic writing tree

Part IV: writing your proposal

The fourth part of this book is about how to write the other essential parts of your proposal. Chapter 9 covers writing the other parts of the introduction, including the background and the problem statement. Chapter 10 goes in depth on researching and writing a proposal literature review. Chapter 11 introduces conceptual frameworks. Chapter 12 explains how to write a methodology/methods section. Chapter 13 is about writing a project plan, and Chapter 14 covers how to cite and reference correctly.

6 *Introducing the doctoral proposal*

Part V: after submitting your proposal

The final part of this book provides advice on the next steps after you submit your proposal. Chapter 15 explains how to give a presentation on your proposal. Chapter 16 explores writing another proposal, which covers both revising a proposal and writing an extended proposal, which is required in some institutions. Chapter 17 covers planning and managing your research. Chapter 18 explains how to manage your supervisory relationships, and Chapter 19 introduces the next tasks to focus on after you have submitted your proposal.

References

Bailey, S. (2018). *Academic Writing: A handbook for international students*. 5th edn. Abingdon: Routledge.

Gillett, A. (2021) *Using English for Academic Purposes for Students in Higher Education: Academic writing*. Available at: http://www.uefap.com/writing/writfram.htm.

Hemingway, P. and Brereton, N. (2009) *What Is a Systematic Review?* 2nd edn. What is …? series (NPR09/1111). *Hayward Medical Communications*, 2, pp. 1–8.

1 The doctoral journey

The doctoral opportunity and challenge

Doing a doctorate is a major undertaking which requires commitment and perseverance. Whilst no one is disqualified from attempting by their age, gender, a disability, or personal circumstances, success often depends upon fitting the doctoral challenge around other life commitments. If you are not at a stage where this is practical, you are advised not to start.

Although you are not expected to be fully knowledgeable and capable when you start a doctorate, you need to have a basic understanding of the subject area relating to your chosen topic. Moreover, you need to be teachable and correctable so that your supervisory team can help shape you into a successful researcher. You also need to have some interest and passion for your chosen research subject as this is the inspirational reserve you will need to draw on in difficult moments.

There are likely to be many highs and lows in your doctoral journey. Your supervisors are there to support you through the lows. Some students overthink their journey when they start and overly focus on outputs and quantity, rather than **quality**. The doctoral journey involves development and self-discovery as well as the production of outputs. Others see the thesis production process too simplistically and fail to realise the complex task management required.

Another important aspect of your journey is the role of the **research community**. Your chosen topic should be of relevance and interest to a specific research (or possibly practitioner) community. You should seek to understand your position within this community and your findings should be of value to them. You should be looking for ways to engage with others right from the beginning.

Phases of a research project

The research process can be characterised by five overlapping phases (compare with Polit and Beck, 2020):

Conceptual: develop, clarify and present a research topic
Critical: review literature, select methodology and method, and design a data collection instrument
Action: collect and organise data
Analytical: analyse data and generate findings
Creative: discuss the significance of findings, conclude and recommend, and assemble final report

DOI: 10.4324/9781003434344-3

8 Introducing the doctoral proposal

Doctoral research projects often follow these five phases, although the action phase may be repeated several times in some studies. This book covers the first phase and the start of the second phase.

The preparation of a doctoral proposal incorporates most of the first phase and the start of the second phase (see Figure 1.1). However, it is common practice for research topics to continue to evolve even after a proposal has been submitted and approved.

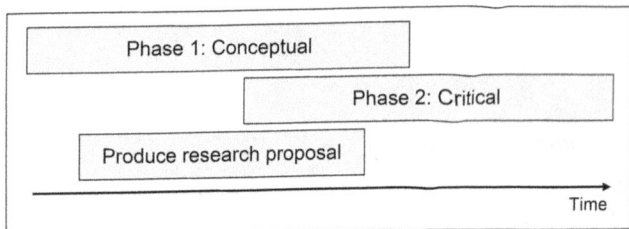

Figure 1.1 Relationship between production on a research proposal and the first two phases of a research project

Benefits of undertaking a doctorate

Here are seven benefits of undertaking a doctoral degree:

- **Deeper knowledge of your subject area:** doing a doctorate should make you an expert in the subject area of your chosen topic.
- **Improved critical thinking:** developing a greater ability to think critically is one of the main benefits of undertaking a doctorate and may be considered more important than your knowledge of your subject area as it is applicable to other subject areas.
- **Improved academic writing:** acquiring the ability to write in an academic style is potentially life-changing and can open doors to your future career.
- **Improved self-management:** a doctoral research project is a complex task which requires managing multiple activities. Successfully obtaining a doctorate indicates that you are able to manage yourself and your time in a complex project.
- **Establish a stronger identity within a research community:** whilst you may already have presented your work in an academic setting and have publications, achieving a doctorate will elevate your status within the research community of your chosen discipline.
- **Improved employment prospects:** achieving a doctorate will make you more employable, especially in academic vocations.
- **Opens door to postdoctoral research:** a specific vocation for which a doctorate can open doors for you is postdoctoral research, especially within your subject area or a subject area similar to your chosen research area.

Reference

Polit, D. and Beck, C. (2020). *Essentials of Nursing Research: Appraising Evidence for Nursing Practice.* 10th edn. Amber, PA: Lippincott Williams & Wilkins.

Part II
Selecting and presenting your topic

2 Selecting your topic

Introduction

Coming up with a good topic idea is one of the hardest parts of the proposal writing process and maybe also the most important. The education system in most countries is focused on developing **convergent thinking** (Robinson, 2010). However, topic selection involves creativity which includes **divergent thinking**. Selecting a good topic also involves reading, evaluating and identifying a viable data source as shown in Figure 2.1.

We shall explore these aspects in turn in the rest of this chapter.

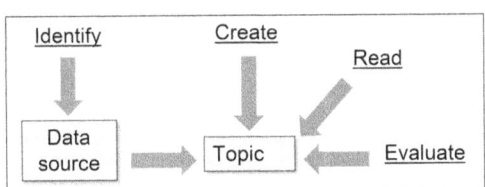

Figure 2.1 The topic selection process. Source: Samuels (2021)

The creative process

As mentioned above, the creative process involves both divergent and convergent thinking. It is the divergent aspect which many students find disturbing. Creative breakthroughs often come unexpectedly. After making a breakthrough, there is still often a validation stage to confirm that the idea can work.

The most widely accepted model of the creative process was proposed by Poincaré (1908) and widely accepted by other researchers (Lubart, 2001). It has the following four stages:

- **Preparation** – conscious work on a problem
- **Incubation** – unconscious work
- **Illumination** – a sudden insight (known as a **gestalt**)
- **Verification** – a second phase of conscious work to shape the insight

The preparation stage

For topic selection, the **preparation stage** involves identifying the scope of possible thesis topics and some key concepts or areas of interest. These concepts or areas can lead to

DOI: 10.4324/9781003434344-5

12 Selecting and presenting your topic

identifying keywords which can be entered into **Google Scholar** (https://scholar.google.co.uk/) as search terms.

Google Scholar is a really useful tool to use at this stage. Later on in the literature search, we recommend using the front search engine from your university library or specific databases. Google Scholar prioritises the sources with the best match and also those considered to be the most important academically as measured by their **citation rate** (the number of citations obtained per year).

Example

A master's student is interested in exploring the implementation of new information and communication technology (ICT) systems in small and medium sized enterprises (SMEs) in the Nigerian retail sector. This could lead to a Google Scholar search using the following keywords, *ict, retail, sme* and *nigeria*, giving the result shown in Figure 2.2.

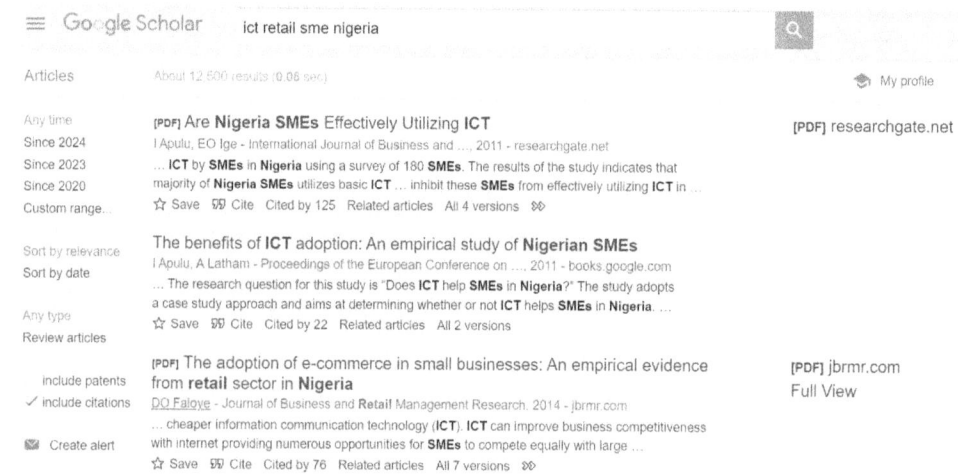

Figure 2.2 Output from the first Google Scholar search

There are about 12,500 matching articles (or **hits**). The first hit has received 125 citations since 2011 (i.e. in 13 years). The second hit has received 22 citations in 13 years. The third hit has 70 citations over 10 years. So the citation rate of the first article is the highest. The first and the third articles are available as pdfs but the first one may require creating an account with ResearchGate, an academic social networking site (https://www.researchgate.net/), before you can access them. The first article is about ICT usage in Nigerian SMEs. The second article is about the use of ICT in accounting systems in Nigerian SMEs in general. The third article is about the adoption of e-commerce in the Nigerian retail sector, which seems to be the most relevant to student's topic of interest.

In order to emphasise the need to identify articles specifically concerning retail, a second search was undertaken with the following search terms: *ict*, "*retail sector*," *sme*, and *nigeria*. Putting quotation marks around the phrase *retail sector* limits the search to articles which match this whole phrase. The results of the search are shown in Figure 2.3.

Selecting your topic 13

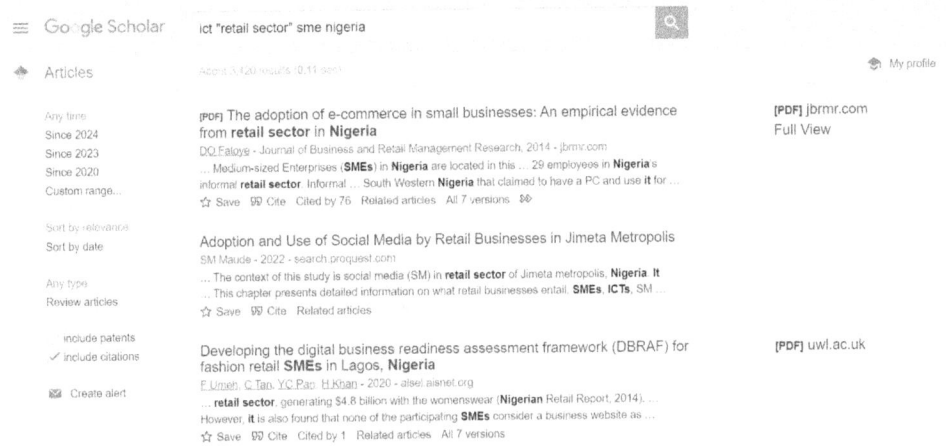

Figure 2.3 Output from the second Google Scholar search

This second search returned with over 3,000 hits. The first hit is the third one in the previous search and seems to be a good match. It has a good citation rate, was published in the last 10 years and is available as a pdf. It would therefore seem to be a good article for the student to download and read. The subject is a particular kind of ICT system (e-commerce) and seems to be limited to small retail businesses rather than medium sized ones. However, it would require further reading to know exactly what definition is being used and how relevant it is to the student's initial idea.

The goal at this stage is not to be systematic in the literature searching, but rather to find some relevant research articles to establish what has already been studied and what is already known about the field. Clearly, the scope of the student's proposed research is currently too broad to be unique as there appear to be several articles already published on this subject.

The preparation phase ends with obtaining a few relevant research articles and reading the most relevant parts of them. The goal of the next two stages is for the student to identify a unique topic that they can realistically investigate.

The incubation and illumination stages

The **incubation stage** is hard to explain in detail as it involves the subconscious. The best time for this is when you are asleep, relaxing, or thinking about something completely different. Talking through your ideas with other people, writing down your reflections, or doing something recreational without a high verbal content (such as playing sport, cooking, listening to music, playing an instrument, or doing some physical exercise) might also help stimulate this process.

The outcome of the incubation process is the **illumination stage**. This is where the reading in the preparation stage and the stress caused by understanding that the topic needs to be focused and practical causes an idea to form in your mind.

The importance of data

The other part of Figure 2.1 we have not yet covered is the identification of a data source. This is critical for selecting a good topic. Your thesis should essentially be about **identifying, obtaining and systematically analysing data**.

Example

Following on from the previous example, the supervisor asked the student why she was interested in the implementation of ICT systems in Nigerian retail SMEs. She replied that it was because of her family business and the examples of good practice she had seen in UK retail SMEs and she was wondering what might be applicable in Nigeria. This enabled the supervisor to identify one source of data – the family business in Nigeria, which could be framed as a **case study**. Another possible source of data would be the retail SMEs in the UK that the student admired, but these might require a different form of data collection.

This helps to narrow down the student's topic to one specific retail SME in Nigeria along with a comparison with retail SMEs in the UK.

Other topic selection strategies

Horn (2012:12–17) suggests some other topic selection strategies:

- **Career goals** – if you know what career you want to get into after you graduate, this strategy involves making contacts with people already working in this area. It could take the form of finding out more about what they do or how they managed to end up in their roles. Your thesis then becomes a vehicle for building a network and promoting your interest in working in this field. This can be particularly useful in the creative industries where many opportunities arise through relational networking rather than traditional job advertising.
- **Solving a practical problem** – if you belong to a social group, such as a place of work or leisure, then you may have identified something which could be improved in the way they operate. This strategy means using your thesis to precisely define what the issue is that needs to be improved and then designing a solution. You might also implement and evaluate a solution: this is known as **action research**. However, when you present your topic in your proposal (see Chapter 9), it should be in the form of a problem that needs to be solved, not a solution you have already come up with.
- **Tutor-driven** – when applying for a doctorate you might look at the research profiles of potential supervisors. Looking at their research interests and what they have already published could be the basis for selecting a topic which might be of interest to them and hence improve your chances of a good supervisory relationship.
- **Using Artificial Intelligence (AI)** – although it is unethical to copy and paste AI generated topics, AI programs, such as ChatGPT (https://chat.openai.com/), can be used in the process of brainstorming topic ideas. It is important to evaluate any suggested topics as explained below.

Qualities of a good topic

Here are some qualities of a good topic (see also Horn, 2012:19):

- It **relates to theory** (a theory is **a recognised system of related concepts which explain how something works in a general sense**) – you should not choose a topic that is entirely practical – you need to be able to theorise what you are planning to do in some way.
- It can be **defined concisely** (see Chapter 3)
- It should be **achievable** within the time frame available.
- It should be **feasible to access the data** – see above.

- It should comply with your university's regulations (such as ethical and safe data collection).
- It should have some **element of originality** – this is often achieved through unique data being analysed. You should also search the literature to ensure that you are not replicating someone else's work exactly.
- Finally, you should personally find it **interesting** – this is very important later in the research process as interesting topics foster **intrinsic motivation** which can help you to have **finishing energy**.

Evaluating whether your topic idea has these qualities aligns with the **verification** stage of the creative process introduced above.

Exercise

David is interested in researching into biology education in secondary schools in Tanzania. In particular, he is interested in the teaching and learning of invertebrates, the use of an inquiring pedagogy, and the role of the English language in biology education. Devise some search terms in Google Scholar so that you can identify the most relevant recent research articles for him.

Summary

Topic selection often feels like a somewhat random, chaotic, or haphazard process. This can be disturbing if you are used to being told what to do, especially as it comes at the start of your doctoral research. It is important to do this well because the overall success of your doctorate often depends directly on the quality of your chosen topic.

Often your first idea will not work. It is important to be patient and give time and space for your subconscious to work. If you realise that you have to change your initial idea, try to **modify** it rather than starting over again from scratch.

References

Horn, R. (2012) *Researching and Writing Dissertations: A Complete Guide for Business and Management Students*. 2nd edn. London: CIPD.

Lubart, T. I. (2001). Models of the creative process: Past, present and future. *Creativity Research Journal*, 13(3-4), pp. 295–308.

Poincaré, H. (1908). L'invention Mathématique, *Bulletin de la Societe Astronomique de France et Revue Mensuelle d'Astronomie, de Meteorologie et de Physique du Globe*, 22, pp. 389–399.

Robinson, K. (2010) *Changing Education Paradigms*. [video] RSA Animate. https://www.ted.com/talks/ken_robinson_changing_education_paradigms

Samuels, P. C. (2021) Dissertations in 20 steps – a Platonic discussion. Technical Report. *ResearchGate*. Available at: https://doi.org/10.13140/RG.2.2.19900.97920

3 Writing your front matter

Introduction

Front matter is the name I use for **the essential information that defines your research topic**. This is your **title**, your **aim**, your **objectives** and your **research questions**. Each of these has its own style of writing (known as its **genre**). They also need to be **consistent** with each other in meaning. The relationship between them is shown in Figure 3.1.

We shall explore each of these in turn.

Writing your title

Your title should describe your topic clearly and concisely. It should not be more than about 20 words long. It should also indicate the context for your research in some way so that the reader can see that it can be achieved in the timescale available.

Example

Table 3.1 provides an evaluation of the titles of the five example proposals (see the Acknowledgement in the Preface for more information).

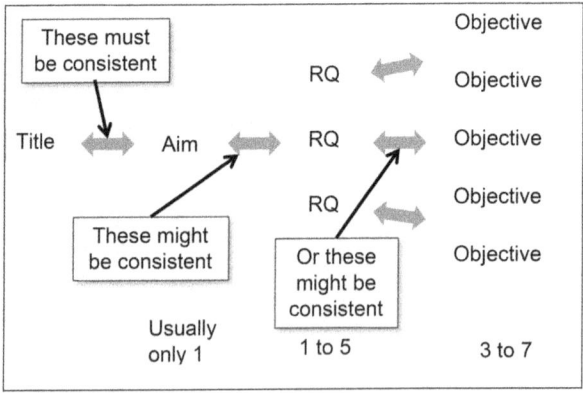

Figure 3.1 Relationship between title, aim, research questions and objectives

Table 3.1 Example proposal titles and their evaluation

Proposal	Title	Evaluation
David	Potential use of inquiry pedagogy on the English language in teaching and learning about invertebrates in Tanzanian secondary schools	There seems to be a slight grammatical problem with David's title in the phrase "use of inquiry pedagogy on" as it is clearly not being applied to the English language; it is presumably being applied to invertebrate education provided in English. The word "Potential" at the start could also be replaced with "Investigating the." The title could also explain that invertebrate education is part of biology education, such as referring to the former as a case study. Otherwise, the scope of his research is appropriate for a doctorate.
Dominique	Non-experimental panel econometric analysis of the impact of social protection: Case study of Rwanda Vision 2020 Umurenge Programme	There seems to be something missing from Dominique's title: what is the impact of social protection being measured? It is not clear what the case study means – how will the panel analysis be constructed? Why is there a need to describe the analysis as non-experimental? Would an experimental analysis have been conceivable in this context? However, overall, his title appears to be of appropriate scope for a doctoral study using secondary data.
Esther	Designing a Footwear System for Persons with Disabilities in Kenya	Whilst a design-based doctorate is acceptable in Esther's discipline, her title is overly concise. It would have been helpful if Esther had unpacked what a footwear system is and who it is for. This would help the reader to evaluate whether the scope of her research is appropriate. The disabilities presumably refer to the need for specialist footwear, so they are physical and of particular kinds. Maybe the emphasis should be on specialised footwear, not the disabilities of the people for whom they are targeted.
Hashituky	Examining Rwandan Preservice Secondary Mathematics Teachers' Mathematical Knowledge to Enhance Algebra Education	Hashituky's title appears too broad in scope. Secondary level algebra education is a wide research area. It would have been better if he had chosen a more specific area of algebra education, such as quadratic equations. The verbs *examine* and *enhance* also do not seem to be the best choice – perhaps the study is intended to be about the relationship between teachers' knowledge and the quality of the education they provide. Presumably, secondary teachers already have the necessary mathematical knowledge to teach their subject (unless they did not study mathematics at this level). But perhaps overly educated teachers do not make the best educators.
Lee	Business Model Transformation incorporating Lean philosophy in a medium sized manufacturing company with high product value, low volume and significant variety	I like Lee's description of his case study manufacturing company rather than naming it. However, I think the phrase "incorporating lean philosophy" could have been improved, for example, to "Implementation of a lean business model transformation".

Writing your aim

Your aim should explain what you are seeking to achieve in your research study. A good word to start your aim is "to" as this forces it to be expressed using a verb. It should be consistent with your title, but it can explain the context of your work in a little more depth. A suggested maximum length for an aim statement is two sentences or up to 40 words.

Example

Here is Lee's aim:
> *The overall aim of this work is to develop a new business model utilising Lean principles to reduce the cost and lead time of manufacturing Rotary Friction Welding machines to enable TFW to remain competitive in the global market place.*

Here are some observations on Lee's aim:

- Lee's aim is about the right length and is correctly written as an action.
- Lee has provided slightly different information about his proposed study in his aim compared with his title. For example, he has given the name of the company and the type of machine which has the characteristics mentioned in the title. These details are complementary, so perhaps he should have included the title information here again.
- Lee's aim indicates that he is only planning to develop a lean manufacturing model in this context, rather than actually transforming the company's business by testing it out and validating it. This is somewhat disappointing for a DBA student, as it indicates he may not yet have fully grasped the nature of active research methods.

Writing your objectives

Your objectives should be more specific than your aim. They should explain **how** your aim is going to be achieved. This means that **carrying out all of your objectives should mean that you have achieved your aim or answered all of your research questions**. Like your aim, your objectives should be written as actions, so it is best to start them with the word "to."

Objectives should all be specific to your context. They should also be written in a logical order. There are two main ways this can be achieved:

1 By splitting up the content of your aim into different conceptual aspects
2 By considering the different stages of the process of carrying out your research and alluding to these indirectly

Example

Here are Esther's objectives:

- To determine how persons with disabilities in Kenya obtain footwear and how involved they are within value chains currently making their footwear.
- To identify footwear crafting, manufacturing and customizing practices that can be adapted to design a system of footwear for persons with disabilities.

- To establish technologies employed in footwear crafting, manufacture and customization which can be adapted to design a system of footwear for persons with disabilities.
- To propose a system that empowers and transfers skills towards persons with disabilities to assemble their own footwear where possible and acceptable.

Here are some observations on Esther's objectives:

- These objectives follow a logical sequence and are quite detailed.
- Esther's first objective sounds really well thought out, but it just needs a little refinement in terms of its language. For example, the phrase "specialised footwear for physically disabled people in Kenya" might be more accurate.
- Her second objective is also very good and goes some way to explaining the meaning of the overly concise title. However, the phrase "system of footwear" is still unclear to a non-specialist reader. Is it equivalent to the "crafting, manufacturing and customizing practices" mentioned earlier? If so, it could have been omitted.
- Her third objective is also good as it follows in a logical order, but again it might be improved by a little refinement. Does the word technologies refer to industrial machines or digital technologies or both? Again, maybe the system element of this objective might be better left out until the last one.
- Her fourth objective is where I suggest she introduces the concept of the system in a way that its link with the previous three objectives is clearer. The other aspects of this objective may be a social ambition, but they are not a research objective. It should not be assumed that creating such a system would necessarily empower disabled people, as its success or failure might depend on other unknown factors.

Writing your research questions

Research questions are the questions that the study is seeking to answer. Some studies have several research questions whilst others have a main research question which is split into sub-questions. For a proposal, a main research question that is consistent with the title and the aim is sufficient. Alternatively, the research questions might be consistent with the objectives written in the form of questions.

Examples

David's research questions are:

1. What are the present language pedagogical strategies used in teaching and learning the biology of invertebrates in Tanzanian secondary schools?
2. What is the effectiveness of IBL in teaching and learning about invertebrates to support learners with language in Tanzanian secondary schools?
3. What is the contribution of the IBL in addressing language barriers in learning about invertebrates among Tanzanian secondary school students?

Here are some comments on David's research questions:

- David's objectives are good because they all mention his research context.

- David's first question is rather descriptive. The current situation is likely to be quite standard (e.g. rote learning, lack of kinesthetics or innovative teaching methods). Perhaps a more important question would be to evaluate how well it is currently working as there would be little point in trying to improve something which is already working well.
- David's second question is quite complex and could be interpreted in different ways. It might have been better to have introduced the concept of Inquiry-Based Learning (IBL) in a question first without mentioning language learning (presumably English). Perhaps an initial question should be how to design a potentially effective intervention using IBL?
- David's third question does not seem to follow a logical sequence as it is looking at language barriers behind biology education. It would make sense to identify these first before trying to design an intervention to address them.

Exercises

1. Improve the grammatical phrasing of David's title.
2. Add some more detail to Esther's title to try to better explain what she means by a footwear system based on how you think she has explained this in her objectives.
3. Write aims for David and Esther based on your revised titles and the information provided in their objectives or research questions.
4. Design some objectives for David's study based on his title and research questions and the comments on them.
5. Design some research questions for Esther's study based on her title and objectives and the comments on them.

Summary

Your front matter is the most important part of your proposal. Each aspect of it has its own genre. You should ensure that you follow the correct genre and also make each part clear and consistent with the other parts.

Part III
Academic writing

4 Structuring your proposal

Introduction

A proposal is a structured document. As the emphasis of this book is on providing a clear and concise argument for your reader, we recommend that you refer to it as containing **sections** rather than **chapters**.

We recommend only using a **two-level structure** of sections and subsections. Over-using a three-level structure of sections, subsections and subsubsections is too much structure for a concise proposal. Not every section needs to be divided into subsections.

This also affects your **argument structure** – if you over-structure your document, it becomes difficult to include deeper writing, especially in your literature review. You should therefore **avoid single paragraph portions** of text. Each portion of text should ideally be **between two and seven paragraphs long**. Anything longer than this makes it difficult for the reader to follow your thread of argument based on Miller's (1956) *seven plus or minus two* rule of working memory. Paragraph writing is explained in Chapter 7. Argumentation is explored in more depth in Chapter 8. Literature reviews are covered in Chapter 10.

Essential and optional elements of a proposal

The essential elements of a proposal are:

- A title
- An **introduction** section including a background, a problem statement, an aim, objectives and one or more research questions
- A literature review section
- A **method and methodology** section (either word on its own is acceptable)
- A **project plan** (this is sometimes included in the methodology section)
- A reference list

These are the elements covered in Chapter 3 and Part IV of this book.
Some optional elements of a proposal are:

- An abstract
- A table of contents (this should come straight after your title page; it is useful with longer proposals)

- A justification or rationale for your study (part of the introduction)
- A discussion on the impact or limitations of your study (part of the introduction or the methodology)
- A conceptual framework
- A dissemination or impact statement
- A budget
- An ethics request form

These may vary according to the requirements of your institution. The only two of these that this book covers are conceptual frameworks in Chapter 11 and budgets in Chapter 13.

Using section numbering

We recommend using a numbering system with sections and subsections as follows:

1 Introduction

    1.1 Background
    1.2 Problem statement
    1.3 Aim and objectives
    1.4 Research questions

2 Literature review

    2.1 Introduction
    2.2 Theme 1
    2.3 Theme 2
    2.4 Discussion

3 Method and methodology

    3.1 Introduction
    3.2 Conceptual framework
    3.3 Methodology
    3.4 Data collection
    3.5 Data analysis
    3.6 Ethics or limitations

4 Project plan
   References

For details on the recommended structure of the literature review and the methodology and method sections, please refer to Chapters 10 and 12. It is useful to use a different font size and a bold font for section and subsection titles. We also recommend that you do not put any text between a section title and its first subsection title.

Example

Lee's proposal follows the recommended structure quite closely (see Figure 4.1).

Contents

1. Introduction 3
   1.1 Background 3
   1.2 Problem Statement 4
   1.3 Aim 5
   1.4 Objectives 5
   1.5 Research Questions 6
   1.6 Contribution to practice 6
2. Literature Review 7
   2.1 Introduction 7
   2.2 Considerations when implementing Lean 8
3. Methodology 10
   3.1 Introduction 10
   3.2 Proposed Research Philosophy & Design 10
      3.2.1 Philosophy 10
      3.2.2 Approach to Theory development 11
      3.2.3 Methodological choice 11
      3.2.4 Strategy 11
      3.2.5 Data Collection and Data Analysis 12
      3.2.6 Study Design 13
4. Impact 15
5. Ethical Considerations 15
6. Plan of Study 17
7. References 19

Figure 4.1 Lee's table of contents

There are just a few small differences:

- He has an additional subsection in his introduction for his contribution to practice. This is appropriate for a professional doctorate proposal, but perhaps it could have been included in the impact section later.
- His literature review needs more structuring. His introduction actually contains a lot of content and could have been split up into an introduction and the first theme. He should also have provided a discussion at the end of his literature review (see Chapter 10).
- There are some issues with the structure of his methodology. There is no need for sub-section 3.2 – this could just have been structured with 3.2 Philosophy, 3.3 Approach to Theory Development, etc.
- The 3.2.5 subsection should have been split into data collection and data analysis.
- 3.2.6 is in the wrong place – study design should precede data collection.
- Ethics could have been included as part of methodology and method.

For more details on methodology and method, please refer to Chapter 12.

Summary

The structure of your proposal is another important aspect of your document as it provides your reader with a roadmap of what to expect. A clear logical structure indicates clear thinking about the presentation of information in your proposal. Numbering your sections and subsections is probably a good idea. You should not over-structure or under-structure your proposal as both extremes have their own drawbacks. As the focus of this book is on being concise, a simple structure like the one presented above is recommended.

Reference

Miller, G. A. (1956). The magical number seven, plus or minus two: Some limits on our capacity for processing information. *Psychological Review*, 63(2), pp. 81–97.

5 Academic writing style

Introduction: busting a common myth

Some students think academic writing is about using long, complex words and sentences in order to impress academics. This is not true: academic writing is about **clarity** and **simplicity**. Words, sentences and paragraphs should be as easy to understand as possible. They should not use unnecessary words or phrases.

The most important issue in academic writing is to **convey your argument as clearly as possible**. We shall be looking in more depth at paragraph writing in Chapter 6 and argumentation in Chapter 7. We recommend watching Foster's (2019) excellent introductory video to academic writing.

Use the third person, passive voice

It is normally good practice to **avoid personal language** in academic writing. This means not using I, my, you, our, etc. This is often achieved by using the **passive voice** to make claims. The passive voice means a person or object is **having something done to them** rather than them being the agent of a particular action.

Examples

Hashituky describes his proposed data collection method as follows:

> The main data to be collected are the written answers to the test items in which they include multiple-choice and the supportive data will be interviewed to probe into their written answers.

His use of the phrase "to be collected" is an example of the passive voice as it hides his identity as the person collecting the data. However, this sentence is rather complex and could have been split up.

David introduces his proposed data collection region as follows:

> This study shall be conducted in the Dodoma region. The region is chosen due to its diverse education institutions compared to other regions in Tanzania. (MoEVT, 2013)

His use of the phrase "shall be conducted" hides his identity as the person conducting this study. His phrase "The region is chosen" hides his identity as the person choosing this region.

28 Academic writing

His use of the present tense for this second sentence is not ideal. His decision was made in the past, but it relates to a future action, so "has been chosen" would have been better.

In her background, Esther writes:

> Historically, people with disabilities have largely been provided for through solutions that segregate them, such as residential institutions and special schools. (Parmenter, 2008)

Her statement hides the identity of the people providing solutions to people with disabilities and it is completely acceptable. It can be assumed that she is referring to certain people in authority.

Later on in her background she writes:

> In this context, the researcher chooses social design as an overarching philosophy for this PhD project.

Esther is referring to herself in the third person as "the researcher." This is not the best way of explaining her choice. She has also used the present tense. She could have hidden her identity by using the phrase "has been chosen." However, her choice of philosophy would have been better explained and justified later, such as in her methodology or possibly in her theoretical framework.

When introducing the proposed location of his study, Hashituky writes:

> A researcher is interested to examine how teachers are prepared before they get the job of teaching mathematics their perspective domain.

Like Esther, he is trying to make his writing appear more objective by referring to himself in the third person as *the researcher*. This should have been avoided here. His personal interest needs to be replaced with an objective argument for why it is interesting which he should have placed in his problem statement. The nature of his research could have been introduced neutrally by referring to it as "the proposed study."

Some dos and don'ts

Avoid contractions

Contractions are the first way in which apostrophes are used in English. These should be avoided in academic writing. Words need to be written in full. Contractions such as *don't, doesn't, hasn't, can't* and *it's* should be replaced with *do not, does not, has not, cannot* and *it is*.

Use possessive apostrophes correctly

The second use of apostrophes in English is to indicate that something or someone belongs to something or someone. This is known as a **possessive apostrophe**. These should be used in academic writing. There are three forms of possessive apostrophe:

- **A single noun not ending in s:** *'s* needs to be added at the end. For example, *Ethiopia's Productive Safety Net Programme*.

- **A single noun ending in s:** either an apostrophe needs to be added at the end or *'s*. For example, either *the business' aim* or *the business's aim* is acceptable.
- **A plural noun:** an apostrophe should be added at the end. For example, *teachers' knowledge of teaching mathematics*. This means the knowledge of several teachers of teaching mathematics. The knowledge of one teacher would be *the teacher's knowledge of teaching mathematics*.

Apostrophes should not be used in any other way in academic writing. A common mistake is to add them to the plural of an acronym. For example, the plural of *SIPOC* is *SIPOCs* not *SIPOC's*.

Introduce acronyms before you use them

An **acronym** is an abbreviation for a proper noun phrase. These should be introduced in full followed by the acronym in brackets. After this, the acronym should be used on its own.

Examples

Lee introduces an acronym correctly in his data collection and data analysis subsection:

> An additional stage in the research will be the development the Supplier, Inputs, Process, Outputs, and Customers (SIPOC)…

> Later he writes: Capturing high-level processes, a SIPOC is a visual tool…

However, Esther introduces an acronym slightly differently:

> Situations that seem extremely simple and easy to a majority of non-disabled people require an entire organized system of support for persons with disabilities, PWDs.

It might have been better if she had put her acronym in a bracket, but she has pluralised PWD correctly.

Common acronyms, such as UK where the audience can be assumed to be based in the United Kingdom, are acceptable. However, do not assume technical or discipline-specific acronyms as your proposal needs to be accessible to non-specialist readers.

Avoid Latin abbreviations

Latin abbreviations should be avoided in academic writing: *e.g.* should be replaced with *for example* or *for instance*; *i.e.* should be replaced with *in other words* or *that is to say*; *etc.* should be replaced with *and so on*.

One Latin abbreviation that you might use is *et al.*, which means *and others*. It is used with several alphabetical referencing systems, such as APA and Harvard. In APA it is used to indicate several authors when a publication has more than three authors. In Harvard style, it is used when a publication has more than two authors. It should only be used in the citation and not in the reference list.

For example, in his literature review, Dominique writes:

> Wheeler et al., (2010) confirm this in the cash/food debate…

This is almost correct. It should be *Wheeler et al. (2010)* – i.e. there should be no comma after *al*.

However, according to his reference list, this source document only has two authors, so in both Harvard and APA styles it should have been cited as:

Wheeler and Devereux (2010) confirm this...

For more information on referencing, please refer to Chapter 13.

Be consistent when writing numbers

Small whole numbers (ten or less) should be written in words whilst larger numbers, numbers with decimals and percentages should be written in figures.

For example, in his methodology, David writes, *around 10 secondary schools under the study will be selected*. It might have been better if he had written *ten* instead of *10*, although ten is a number on the threshold of this change in style.

Later in this section he writes, *The target population will be form four and form five*. Whilst this is correct, *form 4* would also be acceptable as it is a technical term in education. Earlier in his proposal he refers to *grades 1 to 3*, which is another technical term in education. The problem with his use of these two styles is his lack of consistency – he should choose one or the other.

Avoid emotive and journalistic language

In academic writing you should avoid language which inspires an emotional reaction from your reader. Do not use colourful metaphors. Avoid using exclamation marks.

Whilst you are trying to interest your reader and you should have some passion about what you are writing, you need to keep your language neutral and unemotive. You are not trying to sell copies of your work as in a newspaper, so the attraction of your writing needs to focus on the interest, clarity and persuasiveness of your ideas, not on your colourful, emotive style of writing about them.

For example, in his background, Hashituky writes:

If teachers can commit an egregious mistake or have misconception while they are teaching mathematics, these misconceptions are passed on the students.

His use of the word *egregious* is inappropriate as it appears emotive and somewhat prosaic. It could just have been left out altogether as the noun *mistake* does not require an adjective in this context.

Avoiding subjective writing

Subjective writing often incorporates poor style in some of the ways already described. However, the main issue in subjective writing is the **poor quality of the argument**. Specific claims made without evidence to support them are known as beliefs or **opinions**.

Esther uses some subjective writing in her background:

> For almost a decade while working at Bata Shoe Company in Kenya, in the Product Development department which oversees design amongst them footwear design, we would receive a large number of requests to make or modify shoes for persons with disabilities who had foot deformities or disfigurement like club foot, one shorter leg, etc.

She is trying to incorporate her personal experience to justify her research topic. If there had been no published evidence to support her claim, then this would have been acceptable, and she could have used personal language. However, it would have been better if she had clearly signalled her use of evidence from her personal experience, such as keeping it in a separate paragraph. The above sentence is mixed up with third person writing. The start of this sentence is also slightly confusing as it appears to be an objective claim about Bata rather than a subjective one.

You should also generally avoid making **value judgments** referring to your own work. The only place where this should be done in a proposal is in your statement of significance, or impact or the potential contribution of your proposed study.

In his impact section, Lee writes:

> The proposed research will add to the knowledge currently existing on Lean but more specifically around a LVHV production environment where there appears to be limited data at present.

The start of this sentence is rather general and could be contested: there is no guarantee that his study will add to the existing broad body of knowledge about lean manufacturing. It would have been better if he had softened his value judgment of his own work and focused on the low volume high value (LVHV) context. For example, he could have written, "It is hoped that the proposed study will make a contribution to the body of knowledge on lean manufacturing in a LVHV context."

This leads us to the subject of ensuring that claims made are not too confident by using hedging.

Use hedging

Hedging is the process of using an **appropriate level of caution** when evaluating evidence already presented. This is especially important in a literature review. Phrases such as "it may be argued that" distance the writer from the claim being made. Softening the scope of a claim by using the words such as "some," "often" or "most" is also useful.

Examples

In his literature review, Lee writes:

> Whilst there is no standard for what is considered contemporary, this value would be considered current enough for it to be relevant in modern engineering practise whilst being wide enough to give sufficient data for the research.

His use of the phrase "would be considered" softens his claim about his choice of time period for article selection in his review. Perhaps *could* might have been better than *would* here.

Lee also writes in his impact section:

> The proposed framework output from this research could potentially be utilised in other industries and this is work that future students could potentially undertake, further adding to the knowledge within academia.

Lee is making a cautious claim about the possible impact of his study by his repeated use of the word *potentially*.

Summary

Many doctoral proposal writers are developing their ability to use an academic writing style at the same time as drafting their proposals. This chapter sets out some important principles in this developmental process. Academic writing style is clear, concise, objective, consistent and balanced.

Reference

Foster, Z. (2019) *Constance Hale Interview on How to Write Better*. [video] Available at: https://www.youtube.com/watch?v=EUNwRpG_5ql

6 Using evidence

Introduction

All academic writing involves making evidence-based arguments. This is true of proposals. In this chapter, we shall look at the need to back up specific claims with evidence, the need to avoid plagiarism and how to quote and summarise other people's arguments.

Backing up specific claims

Every specific claim you make in your proposal should be **backed up with evidence**. In a proposal, evidence takes the form of cited publications.

Examples

Lee makes a claim in his background:

> The United Kingdom's (UK) economy has expanded by 1.5% in 2018, compared to 2.2% in the European Union (EU) and 3.5% generally globally. (The Manufacturer, 2018)

This sentence contains specific factual information and therefore requires a citation. Lee has correctly added a citation and has used the **indirect citation style** of (institutional author name, year) at the end of a sentence. However, the nature of this claim would seem to indicate that a more academic source could have been cited.

Dominique makes a claim about the Vision 2020 Umurenge Programme (VUP) at the start of his introduction:

> The VUP as a pro-poor programme aims at fast-tracking poverty reduction and improving livelihoods of poor in Rwanda like in other countries. (Gillan et al., 2009; Schultz, 2001; Jalan et al., 2003)

This is another specific claim, so it also requires evidence to support it, but the evidence which is provided appears to be about poverty reduction programmes in other countries rather than VUP. So the claim being made may not be supported. Perhaps this claim is supported by the evidence presented in the previous sentence. This problem could be solved by writing simpler sentences, making it clearer how the evidence provided supports the claims made.

There is also an issue about the number of citations being provided. This should not be excessive. Providing many citations does not make your argument stronger; it just demonstrates an inability to use critical thinking to select the most important supportive evidence. As a general rule, **one or two citations** should be sufficient to support every claim.

Avoiding plagiarism and AI generation

Plagiarism is taking other people's ideas, or parts of their published work, and treating them as your own, or not properly attributing them. Plagiarism is considered unethical, especially in many Western cultures, and may lead to an academic misconduct investigation.

The most common form of plagiarism is **cut and paste**. It is particularly tempting to cut and paste other people's work, especially when you are drafting your own work, but this should be avoided unless you are planning to use a **direct quote** (see below). The way to overcome this is to **learn how to summarise** (see below).

Possible plagiarism can be examined by using matching software, such as Turnitin (https://www.turnitin.com/). Such software will generate a report and an overall matching score. Many universities will use matching software such as Turnitin to check their students' work for potential plagiarism. They may also allow their students to submit their draft work to it so they can check their own work before submitting it. However, there is a skill to interpreting the report generated by this software. **There is no safe overall percentage match score** as it depends on the context of the matches. Generally speaking, plagiarism is longer matches in the main body of your work which are not direct quotes and do not have a citation. For more information, see Turnitin.com (n.d.a).

Recently, **artificial intelligence** (AI) features using large language models have become available in grammar checking software packages such as Grammarly (https://grammarly.com/) and QuillBot (https://www.quillbot.com). It is important that you are aware of and comply with your institution's policy on the use of such software. If you are allowed to use them, it may be without using the AI features or you may be required to cite your use of it. Other AI software packages such as ChatGPT (https://chat.openai.com/) can generate content and are probably prohibited by your institution (although these programs can assist in generating topic ideas as was explained in Chapter 2). It is clearly unethical to generate content using AI software and claim that it is your own work. For more information, see Turnitin.com (n.d.b).

Quoting

Quoting is **using someone else's work word-for-word and providing a citation**. This is the only form of cut and paste which is permitted in academic writing. The way you quote will depend on the referencing style used by your institution.

In his literature review, Lee writes:

> Key to this is communication, training of the workers in Lean and developing a "Help Each Other Culture." (Pandian et al., 2010)

Whilst most direct quotes require a page number to be provided, this example does not necessarily need one as the quoted phrase is a compound noun rather than a longer part of a sentence or sentences.

You should not over-quote in your writing. It should be a tool in your citation toolbox. A rule of thumb is **do not make more than 10% of your citations direct quotes**. Quotes are good in your introduction and in the first paragraph of your themes in your literature review as they enable you to borrow someone else's voice to give strength to your own voice.

Summarising

Summarising is the process of rewriting parts of someone else's work in your own words. It is the most important skill to master when using evidence. Many students struggle with summarising as they feel their own summaries will not be as good quality as the original writing they are using, and they are tempted to draft their own work by cutting and pasting other people's work. This is a dangerous thing to do, as explained above, as it may lead to plagiarism, even if you correctly cite the authors whose work you are using.

The way to summarise and avoid plagiarism is to **start by writing notes**. You might wish to print out electronic articles and annotate them, or just write notes on a separate sheet of paper. You should then put the original source to one side (so you cannot see it) and write up your notes on your electronic device. By doing this you are breaking the link between the language used in the original source and your summary.

You should then check whether the content of your draft summary has the same meaning as the part of the original source you are summarising. Finally, you should ensure that your summary is of an appropriate length for the relative importance of this source and that it flows with the rest of your writing.

Example

In his literature review, Hashituky provides a paragraph on algebraic concepts which contains two summaries:

> Referring to the study investigated towards conceptualizing preservice mathematics teachers understanding of algebraic ideas on two specific mathematical concepts (Seago & Jacobs, 2018), it is found that only 26% of participating teachers were able to get a benchmark correctly. Teachers have identified misconception in because they lacked a solid understanding of the basic mathematical concept and appropriate approaches. in the other study also investigated on teachers mathematical knowledge for teaching mathematics in secondary schools in Rwanda by (Hashituky, 2017), a researcher found that more than 40% of teachers are lacking the knowledge of algebra concepts to explain which methods are appropriate when they are given a task combining all methods, the working and non-working methods to solve for the algebraic equations. Yet, looking at competency-based curriculum (CBC), an algebra content is the biggest branch of mathematics that across in many grade levels of years and it reflects a lot on the non-schoolers knowledge.

Whilst Hashituky's paragraph is one of the few examples of longer summaries in the example proposals, it needs some improvement. The reader should not be expected to know what "the study" is in the first sentence or "the other study" is later on. Why were these two studies chosen? What is the overall paragraph topic? His *Seago & Jacobs* summary could be improved by explaining the context in more depth. Hashituky then provides a summary of one of his own publications, which presumably is more relevant to the context of his doctoral proposal. His self-citation style needs some improvement. In both summaries, he provides a brief explanation of the context plus a headline statistic followed by an interpretation. However, the statistics are in opposite directions and probably relate to different things. There is no topic sentence or overall evaluation of the evidence presented. Please refer to Chapter 7 for more information on paragraph writing and Chapter 10 for more information on literature reviews.

Summary

In a proposal you are required to present an evidence-based argument. This chapter explains how to do this. In particular, you need to learn how to cite correctly in order to avoid plagiarism.

References

Turnitin.com (n.d.a). *Interpreting the Similarity Report*. https://help.turnitin.com/feedback-studio/turnitin-website/instructor/the-similarity-report/interpreting-the-similarity-report.htm

Turnitin.com (n.d.b). *AI Writing Detection Capabilities – Frequently Asked Questions*. https://www.turnitin.com/products/features/ai-writing-detection/faq

7 Paragraph writing

Introduction

Paragraph writing is the most important academic writing ability to acquire. That is why it is emphasised in the academic writing tree picture in Figure 0.1 in the Introduction.

If you can learn how to write good paragraphs, you are more than halfway to becoming a competent academic writer.

In this chapter we shall provide a definition for paragraphs and consider the ideal length of a paragraph and explore a module structure for paragraph writing. Then we shall look at the use of transitional words and appraise some example paragraphs from the example proposals.

Definition

Paragraphs are self-contained pieces of writing made up of sentences. They are a bit like a **mini essay**, often having an introduction, a main body and a conclusion. Paragraphs should be **coherent** and introduce and then develop one single **topic**. They should also make one clear **point**.

In order to allow your reader to distinguish between your paragraphs, you should always **separate them with some blank space**.

Length

In academic writing, paragraphs should cover topics in sufficient depth but not be too long so that the reader can still take them in as a single thought. The ideal length for a paragraph is **about 125 words**. Paragraphs are considered too short if they are less than about 60 words and too long if they are over about 180 words.

Short paragraphs can indicate you are not writing about your topics in sufficient depth. Long paragraphs might indicate they contain multiple topics or are incoherent.

Structure

Whilst paragraphs need to flow from their beginning to their ending, there is no fixed structure. Rather, there are some general principles and guidance for paragraph writing.

DOI: 10.4324/9781003434344-11

38 Academic writing

Introduction

It is good practice to start each paragraph with a **topic sentence**, which makes a general point and introduces the subject that the rest of the paragraph will be about.

A **common error** students make in academic writing is to **put a specific assertion in their first sentence** which is backed up with a citation. There are two problems with doing this:

1. It is unclear what the scope of the argument in the rest of the paragraph is going to be.
2. It is difficult to separate your voice from that of the author(s) you have cited. This is particularly an issue in literature reviews and will be discussed later.

This is why it is a good idea to start paragraphs with general claims not requiring a citation.

Main body

After introducing the topic of your paragraphs, you might wish to explain this further and provide some evidence about this topic or one or more examples. There should be some logical flow to the order you present your sentences. You should ensure that the argument is not too long or complicated, and the amount of evidence you cite is sufficient to support your specific claims, but not too much for your reader to take in. This requires critical thinking to have confidence to emphasise the more important evidence.

Conclusion

You should round up your paragraphs at the end with some sort of conclusion. Sometimes this is the best place to write the main point of your paragraphs. You might link to the subject of the section that your paragraph forms part of. You might reiterate the point you made at the start of the paragraph based on the argument you have presented, or you might create an awareness of an issue you will explore in the next paragraph.

Using transitional words

The argument you present in your paragraphs can be organised or structured using transitional words which often appear at the start of sentences. These act as a "glue" to stick your sentences together, although they are not required in between every pair of sentences. Transitional words can help your reader to understand the logic behind your argument and this makes it flow better.

The clearer you present your argument, the clearer your own thinking will be about the subject.

Transitional words and phrases come in different types. Table 7.1 provides some common transitional words split into types.

Table 7.1 Examples of different types of transitional words and phrases

To signal	Examples
Contrast	But, whereas, yet, still, however, although, despite, on the contrary, conversely
Addition	Furthermore, subsequently, besides, next, moreover, also, similarly
Example	For example, for instance, an illustration of, specifically
Time or place	Afterwards, earlier, at the same time, currently, subsequently, later, simultaneously, so far, until now, while
Conclusion	Therefore, in short, in essence, thus, in other words, in conclusion, consequently, as a result, accordingly, nevertheless
Sequence	Then, next, first, second, third, etc.

Examples

Here is a paragraph from David's literature problem statement:

> Biology teaching and learning in Tanzanian secondary schools face different challenges. At the frontline, most of the biology terms are in the English language and Latin to a certain extent. Teachers are challenged to integrating English language development into instruction (Danielowich, 2007). However, the important aspect of science is the richness of words and terms it uses to communicate and share scientific ideas. In this regard, the key to understanding the subject is first of all to understand its language, specifically the vocabulary it uses. Besides teachers, research conducted on language supportive pedagogy in Tanzania (Barrett, et al., 2014) indicated that students are struggling with the English language itself, then after, with the vocabulary used in biology subject, particularly in invertebrates.

This paragraph is 121 words long, which is about an ideal length. There are a number of small grammatical errors which make its intended meaning a little difficult to follow. The first sentence sets the overall context but there is no topic sentence. However, the last sentence nicely rounds up the argument and makes a clear overall point, although the introduction of the teaching of invertebrates seems a little tangential and might better have been left to another paragraph.

David's argument presented in this paragraph has a clear logical structure. Two of his specific claims are backed up with citations. However, his claim in the second sentence might have benefitted from a citation. Furthermore, he makes another claim in the sentence about the richness of words and terms in science which might have benefitted from a citation, especially as he follows this by inferring a claim in the following sentence. His use of the contrasting transitional word "however" is also questionable.

In view of this, perhaps it might have been better if he had started his paragraph with this sentence, as it seems to be a good topic for his whole paragraph, then provided a citation to justify his inferred claim in the next sentence like this:

> An important aspect of science is the richness of the specialist words it uses to communicate ideas. Understanding scientific vocabulary is therefore of central importance to understanding the subject of science (citation).

Here is a paragraph from Lee's background:

Modern day manufacturing companies can face competition not just nationally, but on a global scale. In this increasingly competitive market, quality is paramount and critically so is price. The United Kingdom's (UK) economy has expanded by 1.5% in 2018, compared to 2.2% in the European Union (EU) and 3.5% generally globally (The Manufacturer, 2018). The Manufacturer (2018) explain that there are various theories for the slow economic growth, ranging from the levels of UK taxation, to weak investment and to a bloated public sector that squeezes out enterprise. Additionally, Sorrell (2016) states that having slow growth influences a company's ability to raise prices and being unable to increase prices means that a company's only way to increase profits is to decrease costs.

This paragraph is also about the ideal length, being 122 words long. It starts with a general statement about competition in manufacturing but then transitions into an argument about the slow growth of the UK economy compared with the EU and globally. He backs up his specific claims in his third, fourth, and fifth sentences with citations. However, his claim in the second sentence might also have benefitted from evidence to support it. Lee's use of transitional word *additionally* near the end of the paragraph is appropriate as it helps the reader to follow his argument flow.

Lee's overall point in his paragraph seems to be his claim in the final sentence, but it appears to have been derived from somewhat circumstantial evidence: just because the UK economy did not grow relatively very fast in 2018 does not justify the importance of trying to decrease manufacturing costs in a UK manufacturing company. His argument based on Sorrell (2016) is valid but the other evidence he provides appears to be more circumstantial: if the UK economy was growing faster, would there be the same need of rationale for him to carry out a study into lean manufacturing? Perhaps the overall point he should be making is that finding ways to decrease costs is *especially* important in times of slow economic growth. He could then have presented a broader argument about the UK, EU and global economic outlook so that his link between these two claims was not so direct.

Summary

Paragraphs are the fundamental building blocks of proposals and academic writing in general. Mastering the ability to write good academic paragraphs can change your life. Each paragraph should be viewed as a separate self-contained thought so it needs to have some depth but not be too long. Paragraphs should have a start, middle and end.

If you have a science background and are not familiar with paragraph writing, you may be interested in my study guide which quantifies them in different ways (Samuels, 2021).

Reference

Samuels, P. C. (2021). *Academic writing by numbers of scientists*. Technical Report. *ResearchGate*. Available at https://doi.org/10.13140/RG.2.2.33951.89765

8 Argumentation

Introduction

Arguments form the backbone of academic writing. Argument writing complements paragraph writing. It is important to understand that there are two main styles of arguments and when they should be used. If you can learn how to plan your arguments in advance, then it can save you a lot of effort.

Two styles

There are two fundamental styles of argumentation known as **single argument/opinion** and **discursive**.

Single argument/opinion style

The single argument/opinion style is **adversarial**. It can be likened to the **council for the prosecution** or defence in a courtroom whose role is to put forward one side of the argument. The argument presented might still contain evidence which challenges the main claim being made, but this is always argued against. The argument is usually presented as a claim from the beginning when the topic is introduced. Supporting evidence is then presented and the conclusion basically agrees with the claim made at the beginning, although it may clarify it somewhat.

The single argument/opinion style argument should be used in most of your proposal introduction as it should describe the background context and provide a rationale (one-sided argument) for choosing your topic. It should also be used in your methodology as your focus should be on explaining and justifying the choices you have made about methodology and method and explaining their application.

Discursive style

The discursive style argument is very different. In terms of the court metaphor, it can be likened to the **judge** or the **jury** whose role is to weigh up evidence on both sides of the argument. A subject is introduced neutrally at the start, rather than a claim about it. Evidence is then presented on both sides of the argument and then a cautious conclusion is drawn at the end which **could not be anticipated** from the beginning.

The discursive style argument is very useful in literature reviews. It enables you to distance yourself from the evidence you are presenting and evaluate conflicting evidence in the process of exploring deeper questions. A common error in academic writing is an overuse of the single argument/opinion style in literature reviews.

Examples

Single argument/opinion argument

Here is an example of an adversarial argument from Esther's literature review:

> Manufacturing has been the prime driver in the evolution of society from one that is agriculturally centered to one that is industrially centered (Boër and DulioMass 2007). Manufacturing technology started with an artisan at work making a single product for a single customer, and as such was well recognized as craft production during the first industrial revolution 1iR. The fourth industrial revolution, 4IR has seen technological innovations take place rapidly in all sectors of our lives. One of the main trends in today's market is that of 'mass customization' which represents a new market paradigm that is changing the way consumer products are designed, manufactured, delivered and recycled.

This paragraph is 108 words long, which is about the right length. Esther's first sentence serves fairly well as a topic sentence. Her point is in her last sentence and refers to the contemporary trend of mass customization of industrially manufactured products. Her argument is all in one direction, providing a chronological summary of the development of product manufacture. This makes it a single argument/opinion style.

Esther correctly backs up her claim in her first sentence with a citation, but she has not provided evidence to support her claims in her other sentences. There is also a rather large leap between the subjects of her second and third sentences which might have been better signalled. She should also have introduced her abbreviations in brackets, e.g. "the first industrial revolution (1iR)."

As this paragraph appears in the middle of Esther's literature review, it might have been beneficial if she had considered addressing some deeper issues regarding this topic, such as the advantages and disadvantages to society of the new market paradigm of mass customization, the possible reasons for its recent emergence, or potential future trends in product manufacture.

Discursive argument

Dominique uses a discursive style argument in this paragraph from his literature review:

> Evidence from different countries, including Africa (Ethiopia, Ghana, Kenya, Lesotho, Malawi, Zambia, and Zimbabwe) show that cash transfer is also known as "Direct Support" overall has a positive impact on household consumption expenditure (Food and Agriculture Organization et al., 2016). Wheeler et al., (2010) confirm this in the cash/food debate using the income and asset growth model on Ethiopia's Productive Safety Net Programme (PSNP). The study shows a positive, but less cash income gains compared to food transfers in the presence of inflation. Also, the joint impact assessment of cash transfers and farm input subsidy programmes in Malawi without indirect benefits factors demonstrated a higher positive and

significant impact than individual programme impact (Pace et al., 2016). However, Zanker et al., (2011) argue against the positive effect of cash transfers on the poor, providing evidence that the results depend on the choice of indicators that best reflect the characteristics of beneficiaries and the targeting. Alderman (2013) also argues against the same claim, stating that in-kind transfers might work better than cash transfers in the same setting. In summary, the choice of indicators and inflation factor might need consideration in the impact assessment of cash transfer programmes.

Overall, this is a very well-written paragraph, although it is a little on the long side (196 words) and Dominique's opening sentence could have been simplified. After his topic sentence, he summarises two studies which argue the positive effects of cash transfer programmes on household consumption. This is followed by the transitional word "However" which introduces a contrary argument comprising two additional study summaries. Finally, a conclusion is drawn which combines details from two of the summaries to identify potential factors when evaluating the success of cash transfer programmes.

Argument planning

Keen students often waste much time by overwriting and then trying to cut down their draft. Other students write what comes into their heads without a plan. This often means not knowing what you are trying to say and leads to your paragraphs being unclear in flow and direction and not making a single clear point.

The answer to these problems is to **plan your argument in advance**.

Here is how to do it:

- For each section of your proposal, calculate an estimated word count based on the overall wordcount and their relative importance. For example, for a 3,500-word proposal, a literature review of about 1,400 words is recommended.
- For sections longer than 1,000 words, decide how they will be split into subsections and calculate an estimated wordcount for each subsection (for advice on how to split up your literature review, please refer to Chapter 10).
- For sections under 1,000 words, divide the estimated wordcount by 125 to give you an estimated number of paragraphs. For example, for our undergraduate students, this would lead to six or seven paragraphs for their literature reviews.
- Now imagine you are giving a presentation to some of your fellow students about the subject of your section or subsection and you have **one slide** to present some **bullet points**.
- Write one bullet point for each paragraph.
- Now evaluate your points: are they in the right order and are they equally important?
- Once you have clarified the points you are trying to make, you just need to draft one paragraph around each point.

By following this method, your argument will be clearer, and you will avoid overwriting. This will also save you time. It will also help you to **socialise your writing process** as you will be imagining someone listening to your presentation of your argument.

44 *Academic writing*

Example

Here is an example of an argument plan presentation for the introduction section of one of my own research papers (Samuels and Haapasalo, 2012). This section is 1,075 words long and is split into ten paragraphs.

- There is a major problem with older students' engagement with mathematics
- There has been a rapid increase in the adoption of new (mobile) personal technologies by contemporary learners
- But the educational sector has been slow to adapt their approaches in view of this increase
- There is also a need to emphasise practices for making informal mathematics rather than formal mathematics
- There have been past successes with turtle graphics robots and the LOGO programming language for teaching basic mathematics to younger children
- Research into whether using physical robots or a virtual programming language is better is inconclusive
- There is a potential application of robotics with older students
- It is now possible to animate virtual robots within richer mathematical environments
- Aim of paper: to combine real and virtual robotics with older students to motivate mathematics engagement and learning
- Outline: rationale; pedagogical approach; evaluation criteria; feasibility and technological evaluation; pedagogical evaluation

This example is slightly on the long side for this technique, but you should be able to follow this argument even without knowing very much about the subject. Try to use this technique to plan arguments between three and seven paragraphs long.

Exercise

Based on the suggested proposal outline from Chapter 4:

1 Introduction

    1.1 Background
    1.2 Problem statement
    1.3 Aim and objectives
    1.4 Research questions

2 Literature review

    2.1 Introduction
    2.2 Theme 1
    2.3 Theme 2
    2.4 Discussion

3 Method and Methodology

    3.1 Introduction
    3.2 Conceptual framework
    3.3 Methodology

3.4 Data collection
3.5 Data analysis
3.6 Ethics or limitations

4 Project plan

Use the total wordcount that you are aiming to write for your proposal to estimate the number of paragraphs you need for each section and subsection based on an average paragraph length of 125 words.

Then create a draft presentation with one bullet point per paragraph to provide the argument structure for your whole proposal.

Then use your plan to draft your proposal.

Summary

Arguments form the **backbone** of your proposal. There are two basic styles known as single argument/opinion and discursive. These styles should be used in the appropriate context. Your argument needs to be clear, make sense and flow. The argument planning technique recommended above can help you to improve your argument, save time and be more considerate of your audience.

Reference

Samuels, P. C. and Haapasalo, L. (2012). Real and virtual robotics in mathematics education at the school-university transition. *International Journal of Mathematical Education in Science and Technology*, 43(3), pp. 285–301.

Part IV
Writing the rest of your proposal

9 Writing the rest of your introduction

Introduction

Now that we have covered topic selection and the basics of academic writing, we can focus on writing the rest of your proposal. In this chapter, we will look at writing the rest of your introduction. We have already covered front matter writing in Chapter 3, so we just need to cover the remaining elements. The most important of these are the **background** and the **problem statement**. Together they form your **rationale**. I begin by discussing these elements and then move on to the other optional elements which you might choose to present later on in this section.

Writing your background

Your background should provide your reader with a basic understanding of the key concepts which are being combined together or applied to create your research topic. You should write one paragraph for each concept which should include **definitions** and **basic factual information**.

A useful metaphor for background writing is the What 3 Words app (https://what3words.com/). This app can be used to pinpoint any 3-metre sided square on the earth's surface by using a unique combination of three English words. In the same way, it should be possible for you to define a unique research topic by combining together three, or at most four, distinct fundamental concepts. You should aim to write one paragraph on each concept.

Another metaphor for background writing is a **big cat scent marking its territory**. Each paragraph in your background and its associated topic is like a tree or rock that you need to "scent mark" by demonstrating that you have a good basic understanding of that subject.

Example

Hashituky's proposal title is, "Examining Rwandan Preservice Secondary Mathematics Teachers' Mathematical Knowledge to Enhance Algebra Education." His background contains four paragraphs covering the following topics:

- The requirements for and benefits of effective mathematics teaching in the contemporary Rwandan context
- Issues concerning the preparation of preservice mathematics teachers and their consequences

DOI: 10.4324/9781003434344-14

- The impact of Rwandan mathematics curriculum changes on student outcomes
- A collection of general questions about pre-service mathematics teachers

As mentioned in Table 3.1 of Chapter 3, Hashituky's title appears to be too broad in scope for a single doctorate. However, his third background paragraph indicates that the contemporary Rwandan context includes a major mathematics curriculum change which would narrow down the scope of his research.

His first paragraph contains useful material but maybe it could have come later or not focused so quickly on the Rwandan context. His second paragraph appears very relevant. However, his background does not mention algebra education, which seems to be a significant omission. In addition, his fourth paragraph contains inappropriate content for a background as it neither defines nor describes any aspects of his chosen topic.

In summary, the following three-paragraph concepts might better have covered his proposed doctoral topic:

- The preparation or pre-service secondary mathematics teachers, maybe with a focus on Africa
- The teaching of algebra in secondary schools, maybe with a focus on Rwanda
- Recent mathematics curriculum changes in Rwanda and their impact on teacher training

Writing your problem statement

Your problem statement should connect your background with your chosen research topic. It should be shorter than your background, so two paragraphs might be sufficient. The argumentation style of your problem statement should be adversarial as you are providing a rationale for why your topic is **interesting**, **relevant**, **original**, and **achievable** as explained in Chapter 2.

One technique for problem statement writing is to combine together the concepts introduced in two of the paragraphs from your background. Another technique is to include the context of your research associated with the data you are proposing to collect.

Your problem statement should also include some citations of studies closest to your own in order to **establish a research gap**.

The conclusion to your argument in your problem statement should be your aim. You should not mention your proposed study until this point.

Example

Lee's problem statement contains three paragraphs on the following topics:

- An overview of Thompson Friction Welding (TFW) and the friction welding process and business environment
- TFW's current implementation of a quality management system
- Potential benefits of the proposed research

Lee's first paragraph contains some useful information, but he seems to go into a bit too much detail about the friction welding process and could have provided more factual information about the friction welding business environment in general and TFW in particular. Alternatively, some of his friction welding content could have been moved to his background as he currently chose not to mention this there at all. It might have then made sense to have introduced TFW in his problem statement.

Lee's second paragraph contains important information for setting the context of his practice-based research. However, he does not provide any rationale for the possibility of implementing lean manufacturing or any citations of similar studies concerning quality management systems in engineering manufacture, the processes they adopted or the evaluation of their success. This would have enabled him to establish his research gap. As it is, this paragraph does not link sufficiently with his background and does not enable him to establish an adequate rationale for his aim.

Lee's final paragraph does not belong in his problem statement – it would have been better if he had discussed these issues after introducing his aim, objectives and research questions. As already mentioned, the conclusion of your problem statement should be equivalent to, or provide justification for, the statement of your aim.

Additional parts

Additional subsections of an introduction you might include are:

- A **rationale** or **justification** for your study – however, there is no real need for this if you write your background and problem statement well. If your institution requires you to write it, then it should just be a short section that reiterates the argument you have already presented in these sections.
- **Thesis** – a statement of what you are trying to show. This is not appropriate in all studies, and you should be careful **not to sell a solution** as you need to focus on the problem you have identified in your proposal introduction, not a solution to it. This might be a single sentence, or it might be up to one paragraph. Furthermore, I would recommend **not including hypotheses** in an introduction as these make assumptions about the type of research you are proposing to undertake and the type of data you are planning to collect, which can only be adequately explored in your methodology section. However, please follow the advice of your supervisors and any subject-specific or contextual expectations.
- **Scope** or **location** of the study – this could provide an opportunity to explain what context will be focused on and what data will be collected.
- **Limitations** – you might want to reflect on potential limitations to the achievement of your aim. However, these might be better placed in your methodology section.
- **Significance** or **potential impact** – these might be relevant here. You should write these **modestly** using phrases such as "It is hoped that this research will be of some benefit to …," or "… make a small contribution to…"
- **Outline** of the rest of your proposal, although there is no real need for this as your primary readers should already know the structure of proposals.

Examples

Esther provides a four-paragraph **justification** for her choice of topic (not included here). However, some of her material might have better been placed in her problem statement as the latter currently lacks any citations to support her argument and is only one paragraph long. As already mentioned, a problem statement should justify the choice of topic

52 *Writing the rest of your proposal*

and establish that there is a research gap. Esther's current problem statement is rather unconvincing and requires improvement. She could still retain a justification section, but it could be shorter and provide supplementary material that she considered was not essential for establishing her research aim.

David provides a single paragraph statement of the **significance** of his proposed research:

> Studies have been undertaken on learners' difficulties in learning the biology of invertebrates and have indicated that most of the challenges they had are related to the language barrier (Danielowich, R007; Grimaldi & Engel, 2005; Heughet al.2007; Prokop et al., 2011). However, little has been done on the use of inquiry-based teaching and learning pedagogy to support learners with the English language in the biology subject at secondary school level in Tanzania focusing on invertebrates. Data on how to solve teacher and learners' language difficulties in learning biology subject will be generated, and then shall potentially impact practice, policy and curriculum matters in the Tanzanian Ministry of Education. The results of the study would equally be useful to educational institutions, school heads, teachers of biology and other stakeholders who may wish to improve classroom teaching and learning. Given its recognized importance, the study would open the door and motivate other scholars to carry out similar research or scale up this work beyond this scope.

The first two sentences of this paragraph are more of a justification and might have complemented his problem statement material, so they are not required here. The rest of his paragraph contains more appropriate content. He correctly uses the word "potentially" to qualify his claim of significance. However, perhaps the word "might" would have been more accurate than "would" in his last two sentences.

Hashituky begins his introduction with a statement of the **location** of his study:

> The goal of teacher education in college is to make teacher trainees stay with knowledge, attitude, behavior, and skills so that they become intelligent users of that knowledge and transfer it to other generations through learning and teaching process. Teachers as they are always required to perform and implement what education policy, researchers and writers have invented, everyone expects them to have mathematical knowledge and reasoning to enhance the quality of education. According to this view, to teach mathematics requires mathematical arguments for ideas that result in meaningful understandings of mathematical concepts. The study will be conducted in Rwanda specifically in the University of Rwanda College of education. Based on periods of which the algebra content is taught, the preliminary data collection will be collected at the end of 2019 and the final data collection will be collected at the beginning of 2020. A researcher is interested to examine how teachers are prepared before they get the job of teaching mathematics their perspective domain.

This may have been required by the template he was using, but it is not generally advised as it is better to begin an introduction with a background which defines and describes some key concepts. Indeed, Hashituky appears to struggle with his use of this section at the start of his introduction, as his first three sentences provide more of a rationale for his research than actually referring to its scope. The additional problem with starting like this is it is inappropriate to make an argument using concepts which have not yet been defined or described. His argument also lacks any evidence to support it. It would have been better if Hashituky had provided a shorter location statement later on in his introduction, beginning with the material in his fourth sentence. This could have been placed immediately after his statement of his aim, objectives and research questions.

Summary

Introductions are another important aspect of proposals as they provide the context for the introduction of your front matter and will be read first. They should follow a simple genre and present the right kind of writing in each subsection. Your argument in your introduction should be clear and flow in a logical order. Try to avoid repetition by understanding the purpose of each aspect of an introduction.

10 Literature reviews

Introduction

The purpose of your proposal literature review is **to provide your reader with a focused critical discussion** of the most relevant research relating to your chosen topic. The literature review is perhaps the most complex section of your proposal to produce, so this is the longest chapter in the book. However, as your introduction will be read first and contains the front matter defining your project, it might be considered even more important. Nevertheless, writing a good literature review demonstrates your understanding of the most relevant published research literature in your field, which is one of the important things proposal markers are looking for.

In most academic disciplines, a literature review in a research proposal should be more than an **annotated bibliography**, which is simply a sequence of single paragraph summaries of research studies. Instead, it should be organised into a few key **themes**, which are broader research areas than your chosen research topic. Your choice of themes could be similar to your paragraph topics in your background. The process of creating a thematic literature review is illustrated in Figure 10.1.

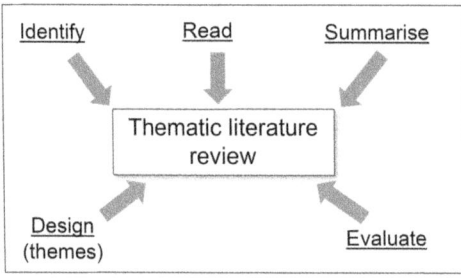

Figure 10.1 The thematic literature review creation process. Source: Samuels (2021)

We continue this chapter by considering some general principles of creating a literature review. Next, we explore how you can obtain suitable research evidence. Next, we will discuss how to choose your themes. It is important to include some theory within your review. So after this we look at different ways of doing this. The main thing that distinguishes a literature review from a background is the inclusion of **critical analysis,** so what this is and how to do it is explored next. Finally, we consider how best to conclude your literature review.

DOI: 10.4324/9781003434344-15

General principles

It is important to **capture your reader's attention** at the start of your literature review. You could consider including answers to questions such as, "Why do you find this research project interesting?" and "Why do you think it is important?" (although your answers should use the third person passive voice).

Your review should start with an **introduction** which states its **purpose** and **scope** and introduces the themes you are going to include. One of the secrets of academic writing is to **answer the question that is in the mind of your reader** without stating what it is.

It is important to **have a plan** of how you are going to write your review. Apart from the steps mentioned below, this should include:

- Moving from a **general** context to the **specific** context of your research
- Using **subsection headings** to structure your review; however, this should not be overdone as it is important to get into a flow in your writing in order to explore deeper issues
- Including relevant **theories**
- Using **visual representations**, such as tables which combine evidence from different sources, or illustrative figures; these will assist your readers who are more visual thinkers than verbal thinkers
- Finish with a discussion that refocuses on your research questions

Obtaining evidence

With the advent of the internet, most literature searching is done online nowadays and does not require entering a physical library. Ways of doing this include:

- Using Google Scholar (https://scholar.google.co.uk/ or equivalent for non-UK-based readers). As already mentioned in Chapter 1, the Google Scholar search engine is very useful in the topic selection process, but it can also be used at the start of the literature search process. Some institutions provide deep links to documents available in their e-library provided that you first log in to them in your internet browser. As already mentioned in the example in Chapter 1, you should use a variety of keywords for the same concept, narrow searches down with quotation marks to create phrases and consider restricting the years of publication, such as in the last 20 years. Once you identify research of interest, the **cited by** link is useful for measuring the relative importance of published research and finding additional articles which cite this article that were published more recently.
- Your institutional library's **meta search engine**. Most UK universities provide a front end to all their electronic resources, known as a meta search engine. This will link to their databases and electronic journals. The same principles apply as for Google Scholar, but you may find that the interface has additional features, but it may be slightly more difficult to use. You may have been trained or there may be training materials available, or you may wish to seek out your subject area librarian to help you use this tool effectively.
- Your institution's library may subscribe to some research **databases**. These are normally specific to certain subject areas. For example, business databases may contain other forms of business publications, such as company reports or marketing reports. The same search principles apply as for Google Scholar above.

- Once you start to obtain some relevant resources, you might also start to identify some **electronic journals** which are particularly relevant to your topic area. You may then search directly within these. A suitable time frame for such a search of empirical studies is **the last 10 years**.

You also need to consider what you are looking for and how to choose the best literature to include. The first thing to decide is the overall purpose of your review. Secondly, you need to decide on the **scope** you will be looking at.

Example

Dominique's topic is a panel data analysis of the impact of the Rwanda Vision 2020 Umurenge social protection programme. When considering what literature to include in his review, he could decide on the scope of social protection programmes to include, such as East Africa, Sub-Saharan Africa, the whole of Africa, all developing countries globally, or those with similar economies to Rwanda.

Once you have identified a sufficient amount of relative literature, you need to decide how to choose what to look at in more depth and then eventually what to include using some type of citation. I like to use a rule of thumb for this which I call the **50-40-10 principle**, as illustrated in Figure 10.2.

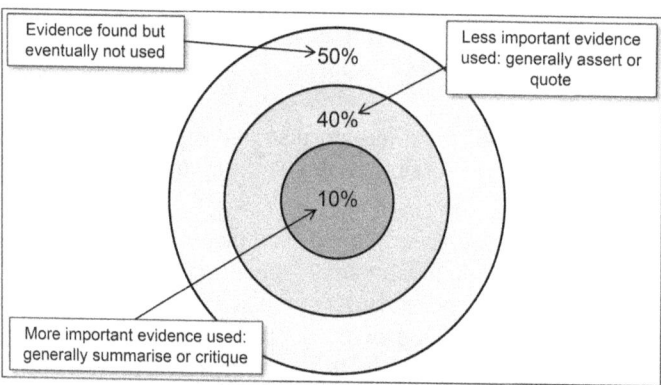

Figure 10.2 The 50-40-10 principle

A mistake made by some keen students is to find and read too much evidence in detail. They end up confused, work too hard and do not get the credit they deserve. The 50-40-10 principle indicates that you should aim to only **find about twice as much evidence as you eventually use**.

A second mistake some students make is to treat all citations at the same level of importance, such as in an annotated bibliography. This will also not lead to receiving credit as it does not demonstrate critical thinking. You should not aim to write the same amount of text about each reference. The most important evidence should have a longer form of citation, such as a summary or a critique. The less important evidence should have a shorter citation, such as an indirect citation backing up a factual claim, a direct quote or a single sentence summary. The ratio of the most important evidence to the least important evidence should be about 4:1.

Another issue to consider is how many references you should have in your literature review. My advice is as follows:

- Your literature review should be about 35–40% of your proposal word count.
- The density of citations in a literature review is normally higher than in other forms of academic writing. I would recommend about 20 references per 1,000 words.

Example

Considering a concise doctoral proposal of about 3,500 words, the length of the literature review might be about 1,400 words (which is 40% of the total wordcount). This is recommended to contain about 28 references. Using the 50-40-10 principle, this would mean identifying about 55 relevant references of which 28 were used and about 5 of these 28 were summarised or critiqued, whilst the other 23 have shorter forms of citation.

Deciding on your themes

Whilst proposal literature reviews should be quite concise, it is still a good idea to split them into **themes**. Themes are broader areas than your chosen topic. They are often similar in scope to the topics of paragraphs in your background (see Chapter 9). Themes can also be viewed as perspectives which have their own literature base. They should be distinct from each other, or they should not overlap very much. The combination of your themes should provide alternative perspectives for viewing your topic.

You may already have an idea of which themes you want to include, or they may become clear from your literature review. A technique I recommend is to **draw a concept map** of your literature review and **create a post-it note** for each of your references (including the author, year and a brief description), then try to **stick the post-it notes** to the concept map (see Figure 10.3). The clustering of the notes on the map might indicate possible themes.

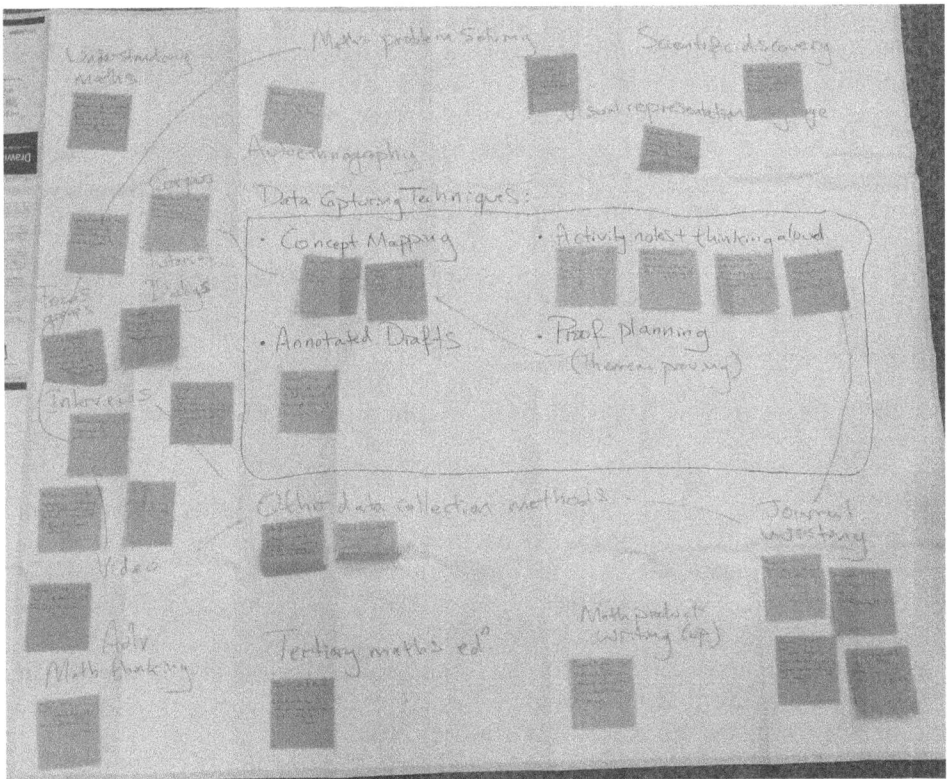

Figure 10.3 Example concept map with post-it notes (from my own research)

58 Writing the rest of your proposal

Your themes should also have an appropriate scope with a sufficient number of references, but not too many.

Example

Dominique's literature review is divided into three themes:

- Direct support
- Public works
- Financial services

These cover his research topic well. However, they were each only one paragraph long, making it difficult to present a deep argument. It might have been better if he had only used two themes so that they could have been longer.

Including theory

Literature reviews should also include **theoretical perspectives**. A theory is a collection of concepts which explain how a phenomenon works. They are usually well regarded in the research community and remain relevant for a longer period of time than most primary research studies (which are known as **empirical literature**).

You can include theory in different ways:

- A theory might be relevant to your whole review. You could then begin your review with a **theoretical framework**, which would become your first theme. You should try to move beyond simply introducing and describing a theory by attempting to answer deeper questions about it, such as "how does it apply to my context?" and "what are its strengths and weaknesses?" Please see the next section for more information.
- There may be one or more theories relevant to one of your themes. You might then discuss these in the first paragraph of your theme.
- You might refer to a less important theory in passing within your argument.

Example

The second theme of David's literature review contains a theoretical perspective in the first paragraph:

> There are different forms of inquiry learning (Feldman & Flores, 2017). One of them is structured inquiry whereby the teacher provides the input for the student with a problem to investigate along with the procedures and materials. This type of inquiry learning is used to teach a specific concept, fact or skill and leads the way to open inquiry where a student formulates his or her problem to investigate. An example of a structured inquiry learning approach is the Learning Inquiry Cycle Model, based on Piaget's theory of cognitive learning (Bevevino, Dengel, & Adams, 1999). The learning cycle model is a teaching procedure consistent with the inquiry nature of science and with the way children naturally learn (Pedaste et al., 2015). Besides the

learning cycle model, there is guided inquiry learning. It focuses on the structure of laboratory experiments as a lesson within cycles. (Feldman and Flores, 2017).

David explains how the teaching method Learning Inquiry Cycle Model is based on Piaget's educational theory of structured inquiry learning. Educational theories explain how people learn whereas teaching methods are prescribed ways of teaching, which can be informed by educational theories.

Including critical analysis

Many students ask me what critical analysis is and whether their writing includes it. A common criticism of literature reviews is that they lack critical analysis. There is a debate amongst researchers and educators on this subject. There are different perspectives on what critical analysis is. My view is that critical analysis is different in nature between different subject areas, but it has some common features across all subjects.

Critical analysis is a specific type of **critical thinking**. Ennis (2011) defines critical thinking as "reasonable and reflective thinking focused on deciding what to believe or do." Critical analysis is **the application of critical thinking to the evaluation of research evidence**. A popular study book on critical thinking is by Cottrell (2017). However, other authors such as Moon (2007) explain critical thinking in a more developmental and less skills-orientated manner.

When including critical analysis in a proposal literature review, a very useful device is a **discursive style paragraph**. This is a single paragraph argument which introduces a subject area, presents evidence from different perspectives and then evaluates this evidence in the form of a cautious conclusion, which uses **hedging**. Please refer to Chapters 5, 7 and 8 for more information on hedging, paragraph writing and discursive arguments.

Example

Even though Dominique's literature review themes are only one paragraph long, he has done quite a good job at including a discursive style argument within them. Here is his first thematic paragraph on *Direct Support*:

> Evidence from different countries, including Africa (Ethiopia, Ghana, Kenya, Lesotho, Malawi, Zambia, and Zimbabwe) show that cash transfer is also known as "Direct Support" overall has a positive impact on household consumption expenditure (Food and Agriculture Organization et al., 2016). Wheeler et al., (2010) confirm this in the cash/food debate using the income and asset growth model on Ethiopia's Productive Safety Net Programme (PSNP). The study shows a positive, but less cash income gains compared to food transfers in the presence of inflation. Also, the joint impact assessment of cash transfers and farm input subsidy programmes in Malawi without indirect benefits factors demonstrated a higher positive and significant impact than individual programme impact (Pace et al., 2016). However, Zanker et al., (2011) argue against the positive effect of cash transfers on the poor, providing evidence that the results depend on the choice of indicators that best reflect the characteristics of beneficiaries and the targeting. Alderman (2013) also argues against the same claim, stating that in-kind transfers might work

better than cash transfers in the same setting. In summary, the choice of indicators and inflation factor might need consideration in the impact assessment of cash transfer programmes.

There are many features to this paragraph which are instructive:

- It is a little long, but just about acceptable.
- It starts with a rather complex opening sentence that partially introduces the scope of the paragraph, but it only presents a one-sided assertion (which is later argued against) and contains too much detailed evidence.
- It then presents evidence from different sides of the argument.
- It uses **transitional words and phrases** (*also, however, in summary*) to indicate to the reader how the argument is developing.
- It is evidence-based. The Wheeler et al., (2010) citation goes into a little depth, but it could have gone further.
- It has a cautious conclusion at the end which evaluates the presented evidence. It uses hedging by including the phrase "might need consideration."

There are other forms of critical analysis, but I believe the discursive style paragraph is the most useful technique for presenting critical analysis in a proposal in a concise manner.

Another important way of viewing critical analysis is to consider the **depth of questions** behind your writing. As I already mentioned, one of the secrets of academic writing is to answer the questions in your reader's mind without stating them:

- **Shallower questions** often start with who, what, where and when
- **Deeper questions** often start with **how** and **why**
- It is recommended that you start with shallower questions then move towards deeper questions

Example

If Dominique was to expand his literature review theme on *Direct Support*, he could address a range of questions in a series of paragraphs such as the following:

- What is direct support?
- What are the different forms of direct support?
- Where has it been used?
- Who was it targeted at and why?
- How was it implemented?
- How are direct support programmes evaluated?
- Which direct support programmes (from a similar context to Domique's proposed study) have been effective or ineffective, and why?
- Is there a relationship between the type of support, the type of beneficiaries and the effectiveness of the programmes?

- Are there any cultural issues which might influence the effectiveness of African direct support programmes?
- What overall conclusion can be drawn about the policy of direct support, especially in the African context?

Concluding your review

You should conclude your review with a critical discussion which focuses on your chosen topic. You can begin this by **summarising the findings from each of your themes** and then applying them to your specific context. There should be a smaller number of references which are directly relevant to your own research which you should cite here.

The summary of the relationship between the main concepts in your critical discussion could be represented in the form of a figure, known as a **conceptual framework**. This is explored in the next chapter.

Finally, you can **reappraise your research questions** from your introduction. This will connect your introduction to the findings of your literature review and create a rationale for carrying out your research project which will lead into your next section.

In other words, you should be arguing:

- This is what I said I wanted to answer (as stated in my introduction)
- This is what is already known about the subject (the findings of your literature review, which are often inconclusive, or from a different related context)
- Therefore, this is why I need to carry out this research

Obviously, you should not use first person language like this, but this is essentially what you should be trying to argue in order to persuade your reader of the importance of your study.

Example

Dominque has the most developed discussion at the end of his literature review. He summarises the findings from his three thematic sections and applies them to the design of a joint impact statistical model to evaluate a specific social protection programme in Rwanda from all three perspectives at once. His conclusion is that further work needs to be carried out in order to establish the most appropriate model. This uses an appropriate level of caution and justifies undertaking the current proposed research study.

Exercise

Use the evaluation sheet in Table 10.1 to assess your draft literature review.

62 Writing the rest of your proposal

Table 10.1 Literature review evaluation sheet

Aspect	Evaluation
Overall length about 35–40% of total wordcount	
Starts with an introduction	
Purpose and scope explained in the introduction	
Rest of structure: two themes followed by a discussion	
Appropriate choice of themes	
Choice of themes introduced/justified in the introduction	
Each theme introduced/explained at the start of its subsection	
Paragraphs have clear topics	
Paragraphs make clear points	
Paragraphs are the right length (60–180 words)	
Use of transitional words within paragraphs to indicate argument development	
Use of hedging (cautious conclusions based on the evidence presented)	
Each claim backed up with evidence	
Length of citations distinguishes between more and less important evidence	
Use of a variety of citation styles (indirect, quotes, short summaries and longer summaries)	
Inclusion of theory (e.g. theoretical framework, theme-specific theories or localized theories)	
Inclusion of critical analysis (discursive argument addressing deeper questions)	
Conclusion of themes	
Overall discussion at the end summarising findings	
Reappraisal of research questions	

Summary

Literature reviews are one of the hardest parts of proposals to do well. Remember that you are not trying to create your final thesis version at this stage. Your reader is looking for a basic level of familiarity and competence in the relevant literature. This is demonstrated by your ability to **address an appropriate scope** of literature, **identify thematic areas**, **select good quality relevant contemporary literature**, and **include some deeper writing** which explores some of your cited literature in more depth. By doing this you will also show your **ability to pose and begin to answer deeper questions** relevant to your chosen doctoral research topic.

References

Cottrell, S. (2017). *Critical Thinking Skills: Effective analysis, argument and reflection*. London: Palgrave.
Ennis, R. H. (2011). *The Nature of Critical Thinking: An outline of critical thinking dispositions and abilities*. [pdf] Available at: https://education.illinois.edu/docs/default-source/faculty-documents/robert-ennis/thenatureofcriticalthinking_51711_000.pdf
Moon, J. (2007). *Critical Thinking: An exploration of theory and practice*. London: Routledge.
Samuels, P. C. (2021) *Dissertations in 20 steps – a Platonic discussion*. Technical Report. *Research-Gate*. Available at: https://doi.org/10.13140/RG.2.2.19900.97920

11 Conceptual frameworks

Introduction

A conceptual framework is more specific to your context than a theoretical framework. It summarises the findings of your literature review and presents them in the form of a diagram. This diagram should represent your evaluation of how the most important concepts relating to your study interconnect. For a more detailed discussion on the distinction between conceptual frameworks and theoretical frameworks, please refer to Varpio et al.'s (2020) useful paper.

Conceptual frameworks are generally an optional extra in proposals. If you are planning to collect primary data, they can form a useful visual bridge between the findings of your literature review and the design of your data collection instrument.

The best place to put a conceptual framework is either towards the end of your literature review or near the start of your methodology/method section.

Conceptual frameworks often come in two forms:

- **Tree diagrams** which split an overall concept into areas and subareas
- **Process diagrams** which connect concepts with arrows

There is no hard and fast rule about how to present a conceptual framework. It is best to **read** relevant research articles relating to your own study and get an idea of an appropriate format from any of these which contain a conceptual framework.

However, if you are planning to carry out quantitative research, it is important to bear in mind that conceptual frameworks contain concepts which may not be measurable. It is only once you have discussed how you plan to measure these concepts in your methodology/method section, and whether this is **valid** and **reliable**, that you should present a quantitative model or hypotheses based on them.

Examples

David presents a conceptual framework of biology education in the form of a **tree diagram** which is shown in Figure 11.1.

David's model provides a simple definition and organisation of the key concepts involved in teaching and learning this science-based subject in an additional language using the innovative teaching method of inquiry-based learning (IBL). It is unclear how he might apply his conceptual framework to the development of his research instrument.

DOI: 10.4324/9781003434344-16

64 *Writing the rest of your proposal*

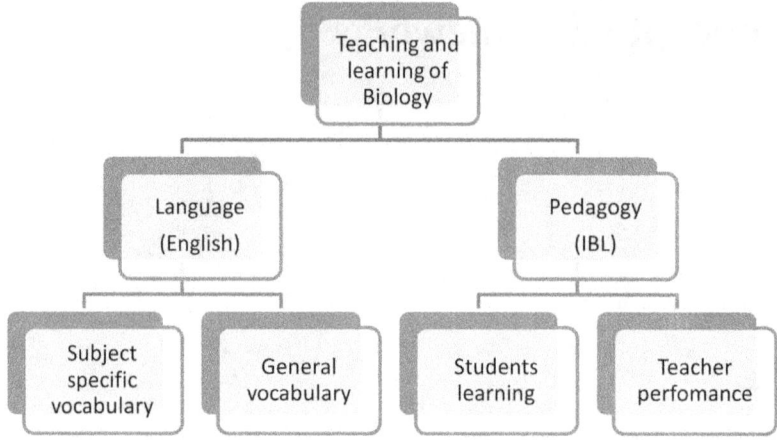

Figure 11.1 Conceptual model in David's proposal. Source (Kaniz, 2015)

Lee provides a conceptual framework for the development of a sequence of prototype rotary friction welding machines as shown in Figure 11.2.

This framework is in the format of a **process diagram**. It prescribes some of the key aspects of developing a high-quality prototype machine within his proposed research study.

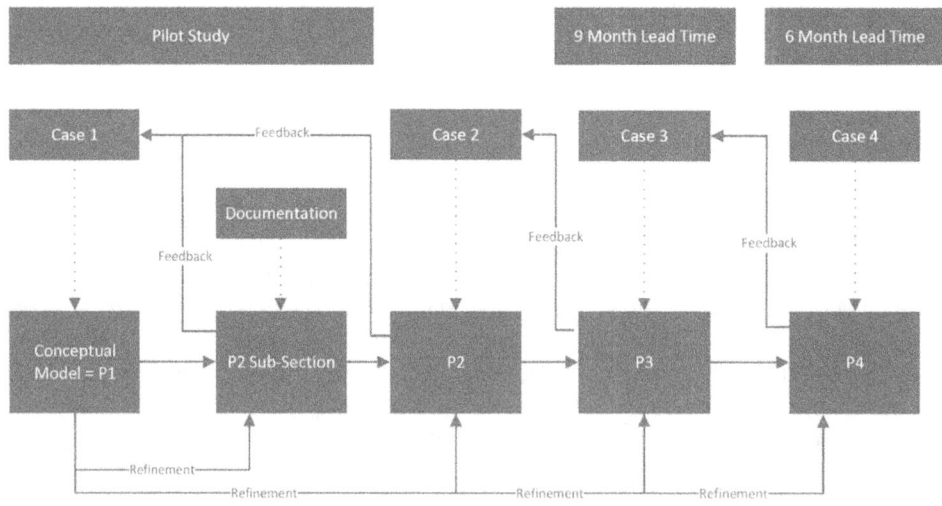

Figure 11.2 Lee's conceptual framework for the development of a series of prototype rotary friction welding machines over the course of his doctorate

Exercise

Create a diagram which describes the relationship between the main concepts relevant to your chosen topic. How does this compare with conceptual frameworks in studies similar to your own?

Summary

Conceptual frameworks provide a useful bridge between your literature review and your methodology/method section. They summarise your literature review findings in visual form and provide a roadmap for your data collection in doctoral studies involving primary data collection. They should be considered even in a concise proposal as a meaningful image summarising your provisional findings can be very impactful to your reader.

References

Kaniz, F. (2015). Barriers in teaching and learning process of mathematics at secondary level: A quest for quality improvement. *American Journal of Educational Research*, 3(7), pp. 822–831.

Varpio, L., Paradis, E., Uijtdehaage, S. and Young, M. (2020). The distinctions between theory, theoretical framework, and conceptual framework. *Academic Medicine*, 95(7), pp. 989–994.

12 Writing your methodology/method section

Introduction: why the name confusion?

Methodology and method go together. **Methodology** refers to the **theory** of how research should be undertaken, including its **philosophical** underpinnings, the **approach** to generating new knowledge and the **strategy** used to obtain suitable data. **Method** refers to the techniques and procedures used to **collect** and **analyse data**. Unfortunately, there is no suitable single word which refers to them both at the same time.

Methodology/method sections in proposals are often poorly written. This is mainly due to misunderstandings about the technical terms they involve, or a failure to understand what the target audience is expecting to read. This is another long chapter as there are many issues that need to be explained which you might find unfamiliar.

Methodology and method can be viewed as concentric layers as shown in Figure 12.1. The recommended structure of a proposal methodology/method section is shown on the right-hand side and is explained further below.

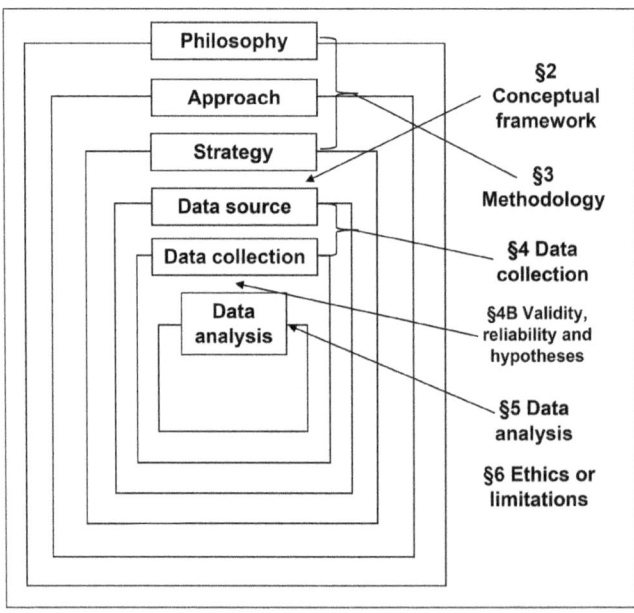

Figure 12.1 Overview of the main elements of methodology and method and the associated sections of a proposal. Adapted from Saunders et al. (2023: 131)

DOI: 10.4324/9781003434344-17

Writing your methodology/method section   67

Your methodology/methods section is maybe the hardest part of your proposal to write well. There are many concepts associated with this section which you need to understand and use appropriately.

Research design

An alternative way of explaining your choice of research is in terms of your **design**. There are three main types:

- **Explanatory** – relating to pre-established concepts, more suitable for quantitative methods
- **Descriptive** – relating to new concepts, more suitable for qualitative methods
- **Exploratory** – relating to a combination of new and established concepts, suitable for qualitative or mixed methods

Please refer to Saunders et al. (2023: 179–181).

The type of design will often link to the type of research questions you are seeking to answer. However, this chapter does not focus on design as it is seen to overlap with the recommended way of presenting your methodology and method in the form of the concentric layers of choices based on Saunders et al.'s (2023) research "onion" as shown in Figure 12.1.

Purpose and argumentation style

The purpose of a methodology/methods section in a proposal is to **present a credible rationale and plan** for the choices you intend to implement in your research. This means your style of argumentation should mainly be a single argument/opinion rather than discursive.

There is a temptation in a methodology/methods section to explain the meaning of different basic concepts. This should **not** be your emphasis as you may assume that your reader already understands them. However, what they do not know is **what methodology/method you have chosen, why you believe it is appropriate in your context** and **how you intend to implement it**. The choices you make need to be **consistent** and **presented in a logical order**. The length of your methodology/methods section should be **about 25% of your total word count**.

Structure

The recommended structure of a methodology/methods section is as follows:

§1 Introduction
§2 Conceptual framework
§3 Methodology (philosophy, approach and strategy)
§4 Data collection
§5 Data analysis
§6 Ethics or limitations

The introduction should mainly explain how the rest of your section is organised.

68 Writing the rest of your proposal

For conceptual frameworks, please refer to the previous chapter. For longer proposals, the methodology subsection can be subdivided further into philosophy, approach and strategy. For shorter proposals, you may need to choose between presenting a conceptual framework and details about your methodological choices.

The other parts of this structure are described in the following sections.

Philosophy

A philosophy is a theoretical way of viewing research and the new knowledge it constructs. According to Saunders et al. (2023: 145–153), some common research philosophies are:

Positivism: This is the philosophy associated with the **scientific method**; it involves observable facts; the researcher remains objective, neutral and detached from the research; it is suitable for quantitative research.
Interpretivism: The focus of this philosophy is on **narratives**, **perceptions** and **interpretations**; the researcher is seen as part of the research and needs to be able to articulate how their identity may have affected their interpretations (known as being **reflexive**); this is the standard philosophy for qualitative research.
Critical realism: In this philosophy, knowledge is viewed as being **relative** and **socially constructed**; the researcher needs to acknowledge their identity, remain as objective as possible, and tries to minimise bias.
Postmodernism: This philosophy focuses on **oppressed and repressed meanings**; the researcher is usually embedded within the power relationships so needs to be reflexive; this is a useful perspective when investigating gender issues, ethnic minorities, disabilities or potential mistreatment of employees.
Pragmatism: The emphasis of this philosophy is on **practical meanings**, **problem solving** and **relevance** to enable successful action; it is initiated by the researcher's doubts and beliefs and also requires reflexivity; it is useful when attempting to improve a process or solve a problem.

As already mentioned above, with a concise proposal, you may need to choose between explaining your choice of philosophy and including a conceptual framework.

Example

Lee provides a paragraph to explain the philosophical stance for his proposed study:

> The proposed research philosophy for undertaking this work is a Positivist approach. The ontological position of positivism is one of realism. 'The positivist epistemology is one of objectivism. Positivists go forth into the world impartially, discovering absolute knowledge about an objective reality' (Scotland, 2012:10). In Positivism the researcher maintains an objective stance and remains detached from the research. This may be challenging in the current study as the researcher works in the company where the research will be undertaken, this is discussed further on in the ethical considerations section. The research will be a case study based in a single company and the data collected will be mainly quantitative data but there will be some qualitative data also. This data will be measurable and come in the form of time and cost metrics.

Lee's choice of positivism is clearly articulated but, as he himself admits, it may be problematic to maintain this viewpoint when undertaking a research project involving people within an organisation. Perhaps he should have considered pragmatism as a more appropriate philosophical stance. Also, going into details about ontology and epistemology may be a little too much for a concise proposal.

Approach

Approach refers to the **way in which new knowledge is generated**. There are three main approaches:

Deductive: the use of data to decide whether a pre-existing theory or hypothesis is true or false; this is associated with quantitative research
Inductive: the process of establishing new knowledge from collected data; this is associated with qualitative research
Abductive: a process of moving back and forth between deduction and induction, for example, using interviews to establish the questions to be included in a closed questionnaire; this approach is associated with mixed methods research where two techniques are used one after the other

For more information, please refer to Saunders et al. (2023: 154–161).

Example

Lee provides a paragraph explaining his approach:

> This research will not be testing an existing theory, as currently when implementing Lean there is no appropriate framework for implementation at TFW. Generally, all companies differ in the Lean tools and principles they apply and the key performance indicators they use to measure them. Additionally, as described in section 2.2, lack of precisely identified needs and the reason for implementing Lean were identified as key roles in the failure of Lean implementation (Garbie, 2010). If the Lean implementation was a success, there is no way of guaranteeing that two companies needs and reasoning for implementing Lean are identical. Therefore, it would be unwise to blindly use a proposed framework by a different company as guidance. The proposed output from the research outlined in this paper is a framework that can be applied to other areas in Thompson Friction Welding's product portfolio. Therefore, as the aim of the research is to generate a new theory and knowledge it will be using an inductive approach.

Lee's choice of an inductive approach is only mentioned at the end of the paragraph. Induction is usually seen as being incompatible with a positivist philosophy, raising concerns about the consistency of Lee's choices. From the rest of his argument, it appears that he is looking to apply certain Lean tools to his case study organisation in order to optimise production performance. Lee's choice of Lean tools will be informed by their application in other organisations. Therefore, perhaps abduction would have been a better way of describing his approach as it appears to be a combination of deduction and induction.

Strategy

Your strategy is your **systematic means of obtaining data** in order to achieve your objectives or answer your research questions. There are seven main research strategies as explained below.

Strategy 1: surveys

A survey is a **systematic collection of information from a sample of people from a larger population**. For example, this might refer to company employees or consumers. There are three main types of data collection instruments for carrying out a survey:

- A **questionnaire** where the same written questions are given out asynchronously – see Brace and Bolton (2022)
- **Interviews** where individuals are asked the same or similar questions synchronously – see Katz-Buonincontro (2022)
- **Focus groups** where a group of six to ten people join together to collectively explore a research issue – see Katz-Buonincontro (2022)

With a survey it is important to state what your **population** is and how you are **sampling** it. This is the process of **identifying your data source**. There are two main kinds of sampling:

- **Random:** which involves having access to all individuals in your population and choosing a sample from them using a randomised process
- **Non-random:** where you select a sample using some other means

It is important to appreciate that vague data source choices lead to vague findings which are of little value. You should therefore be specific about your population for a survey, but you also need to do some informal groundwork before deciding to carry out a survey so that you can be confident that you will be able to collect the data that you are hoping to.

Note: Some people refer to questionnaires as surveys.

Sample size recommendations for surveys

For a PhD research project, it is recommended that you should aim to collect **between 100 and 300 questionnaires**, carry out between **20 and 30 interviews** or organise **three to seven focus groups**. For a professional doctorate, you may aim for slightly smaller sample sizes. Also, if you are using multiple methods, then your sample sizes can be smaller. Obviously, these numbers are only for guidance and the length of these data collection techniques can vary. You should follow the advice of your supervisors who will be more experienced with undertaking surveys in your context.

Questionnaires tend to mainly have closed questions which lead to quantitative analysis. Quantitative analysis works best when you compare groups or answers to different questions. In order to detect differences and relationships, you will need a reasonably large sample. There are no hard and fast rules about this, but quantitative analysis becomes increasingly difficult and less useful with smaller sample sizes.

Even if you include some open-ended questions, it is often difficult to engage your respondents sufficiently so that they reply in depth. Whilst online or email questionnaires require less resources to administer, the main challenge is often **low response rates** leading to the possibility of **bias** (your sample not reflecting the views of the whole population). If you choose online questionnaires, then this should be discussed as a potential limitation in your proposal.

Interviews and focus groups lead to the collection of rich textual data which will require a qualitative analysis technique. It is important to have a sufficiently large sample to allow some variation between individuals or groups, but not too much data so that your analysis can focus on **depth of interpretation** rather than description.

Strategy 2: case studies

A case study is a **systematic attempt to account for the complexity and depth of one or more cases**. In most circumstances, it is recommended that you only research a single case or a comparison between two cases which has a clear rationale behind their choices.

It is sometimes difficult to decide whether to frame a research project as a survey or as a case study. The population associated with a survey might belong to a single geographical area or organisation, which might lend itself to a case study. However, the main distinction between a survey and a case study is that case studies seek to look at a context from the viewpoint of **multiple stakeholders**, for example, in a business this might be employees, managers, customers, shareholders, and regulatory authorities. Therefore, case studies might include surveys as part of their strategy.

For more information, please refer to Woodside (2010).

Strategy 3: ethnography

Ethnography is the **systematic study of people and cultures** – see Gobo (2017).

Strategy 4: secondary data

Secondary data is the **systematic search, selection and analysis of data collected by others**. This is either **raw data** which you analyse yourself or **published research articles** for which you conduct a secondary analysis, known as a **systematic review** – see Hemingway and Brereton (2009).

Strategy 5: action research

Action research is a systematic, reflective and cooperative process of progressive problem solving – see McNiff (2013).

Strategy 6: experiments

An experiment is an orderly procedure carried out to test a hypothesis. Experiments are more common in scientific contexts but may also be carried out in social science – see Coleman (2019).

Strategy 7: grounded theory

Grounded theory is a systematic approach to analyse, explain and theorise everyday experiences. This strategy is different from the grounded theory approach to analysing

72 Writing the rest of your proposal

qualitative data as it focuses on collecting sufficient data for a new theory about a phenomenon to be generated – see Birks and Mills (2015).

Example

Lee provides two paragraphs on his choice of action research as his research strategy. In the second paragraph, he provides a rationale for his choice:

> From a theoretical perspective action research is the ideal tool for the research project being undertaken. Not only does it empower employees through collaborative work, but it empowers them to sustain the planned changes that will be taking place (Somekh, 2006). Applying Action research in a real-world organisation will be challenging and will require adaptation. The purpose of action research is to promote learning within the organisation. This is done by identifying a problem, planning action, taking-action and then evaluating action, this is known as Kolb's action research cycle (Coghlan and Brannick, 2005). Action research has a second form of action research cycle, this is known as the reflection cycle. This form of research then is an iterative, cyclical process of reflecting on practice, taking an action, reflecting, and taking further action. Therefore, the research takes shape while it is being performed. Greater understanding from each cycle points the way to improved practice (Riel and Rowell, 2016). One of the major challenges when undertaking action research is to engage making the action happen and stand back from the action and reflect on it as it happens to contribute theory to the body of knowledge (Coghlan and Brannick, 2005).

Lee's choice appears appropriate for his context. His rationale is persuasive, evidence-based, and indicates an in-depth understanding of two different forms of this strategy. His argumentation style is adversarial, which is appropriate in this section of a proposal. He has clearly read about this strategy in depth and also reflected upon its application and implementation within his case study organisation.

Data collection

Once you have explained your methodology, you should describe your data collection plans. Some common primary data collection techniques are:

- Questionnaires – see above
- Interviews – see above
- Focus groups – see above
- **Observations** – a systematic personal approach to data collection involving prolonged engagement in a social setting, recording your observations using predefined notations, improvisations to develop a full understanding, and paying attention in a standard way – see Gobo (2010)

For each technique you choose, you should explain **what** it is, **why** you have chosen it and **how** you are planning to implement it. With questionnaires, interviews and focus groups, the choice of questions could be linked to the findings of your literature review through a **conceptual framework**. Your conceptual framework should be presented straight after your introduction to this section as it provides a summary of the findings of your literature review. This acts as a bridge to the design of your data collection instrument.

Writing your methodology/method section 73

If you are planning to undertake a questionnaire, you should also explain and justify your **application** of this technique, such as your choice of format being paper-based, email, telephone or online.

For secondary data collection, you should explain your sources of data and your selection methods, and why you consider the data you propose to collect to be valid and reliable.

Example

Dominque specifies his sources of secondary data in his *Data collection* subsection:

> The research will use secondary data from household surveys conducted by National Institute of Statistics of Rwanda (NISR), including the Integrated Household Living Condition Surveys (Megill, 2016). The critical data required for the study will include information on changes in household expenditure, food consumption levels, agriculture production, changes in housing characteristics, ownership of assets, access to credits, changes in employment growth, education status, utilities, and amenities, among others. These sources will provide mainly quantitative cross-section and twin panel data for both VUP and non-VUP beneficiaries.

This paragraph is very informative and has a citation, but it does include a rationale for why these data sets have been chosen, over what period they were undertaken or why they are viewed as being appropriate and reliable. There is some argument about the data types that Dominique is planning to extract, but it could have been linked to findings from his literature review, such as through a conceptual framework. Domique's use of the words *including* and *include* is useful as it allows him to provide specific information without tying himself down to only using certain forms of data.

Validity, reliability and hypotheses

With quantitative data, it is also often important to discuss the **measurement** of your concepts and how this might lead to testing your theory:

- Measurements are **valid** if they measure what they are supposed to measure.
- Measurements are **reliable** if the same or similar results are obtained when they are remeasured, or a group of questions can be shown to measure the same thing.
- A hypothesis is a statement about the **relationship between measurable quantities**. These may follow on from the relationship between concepts in your conceptual framework. **Statistical testing** is the quantitative data analysis process leading to the acceptance or rejection of a hypothesis.

Example

David provides a three-paragraph subsection on the Trustworthiness/Validity and reliability of his study:

- His first paragraph provides a well-rounded argument for the importance of piloting his proposed four forms of data collection.
- His second and third paragraphs argue about how data triangulation can improve data validity:

74 *Writing the rest of your proposal*

Further, validity can be ensured by many methods, including the triangulation method. Triangulation means using more than one method to collect data on the same topic (Creswell, 2012). This is a way of assuring the validity of research through the use of a variety of methods to collect data on the same topic. This involves different types of samples as well as methods of data collection. However, the purpose of triangulation is not necessarily to cross-validate data but rather to capture different dimensions of the same phenomenon (Kothari, 2008).

In the above regard, the reason to triangulate lies on a view that a single method can never adequately shed light on a phenomenon (Kothari, 2008). Using multiple methods can help to facilitate deeper understanding and increase research data objectivity (Mugenda & Mugenda, 2013). In this research, the instruments will be made in such a way that they can elicit both quantitative and qualitative information from the respondents.

As both these paragraphs are on a similar subject and are fairly short, it might have been better if he had combined them into a single paragraph. Perhaps he has included a little too much material at the start of the first of these paragraphs by means of an introduction to triangulation. The goal of a methodology/methods section is to focus on your choices in your specific context, not to promote one method above another as being objectively superior.

Data analysis

Data analysis will depend on the kind of data you intend to collect:

- Numerical and categorical data will always lead to **quantitative analysis**.
- Textual data will usually lead to **qualitative analysis**.
- A combination of the two will usually lead to **mixed methods analysis**.

Quantitative analysis

This can broadly be divided into descriptive analysis and statistical testing:

- **Descriptive analysis** involves the presentation of **tables**, **charts** and summaries of data sets, known as **summary statistics**, for example, means and standard deviations. You should choose an appropriate representation of your data and provide a narrative to go with it and an informal interpretation of its meaning. You should aim for your choice of tables and charts to represent relationships between your concepts rather than just a single concept. To this end, representations such as **multi series tables**, **percentage frequency bar charts** and **scatter plots** are useful.
- **Statistical testing** is the process of making a decision about a hypothesis you have stated in advance. There are many different types of statistical testing depending on the design of your study, including:

    - Tests which compare a measured quantity against different groups;
    - Tests which compare one measured quantity against another;
    - Tests which assume data comes from a predetermined distribution; and
    - Tests which do not make this assumption.

    For more information, please refer to Samuels (2020).

Example

Dominique provides a four-paragraph subsection titled *Data analysis framework*. His first paragraph is as follows:

> The research will use non-experimental panel econometric methods and other statistical models to determine the level and nature of the impact of VUP and its components (DS, PW, and FS) on living standards of beneficiaries (Heckman and Vytlacil, (2005). By design, VUP is a non-random experiment and does not have the control group. Therefore, following the works of Hartwig (2013), Liu et al., (2010), Gilligan et al., (2009), Boonperm et al., (2007), Schultz (2001), and Behrman et al., (1998), propensity score matching (PSM) and difference-in-difference (DD) are considered more appropriate for the analysis of effects of VUP on intended recipients. The study will thus use alternative instrumental variable (IV) models to examine whether the selection bias on unobserved characteristics in PSM and DD that might significantly affect the results is corrected.

His paragraph clearly presents and justifies his data analysis methods with an evidence-based argument. Perhaps there are a few too many cited articles justifying the use of these two forms of panel data analysis – he could have used critical thinking to cut these down and maybe provided a brief summary of the strongest supportive citations. Using the phrase "are considered more appropriate" is a good use of the passive voice, but it raises the question "than what?" in the mind of the reader, which would require an explanation of possible alternatives. It might have been better if Dominique had stuck to providing an argument about using panel data methods in this paragraph and had gone into more detail about his choice of types of analysis in a separate paragraph.

Qualitative analysis

If qualitative data is very brief, which is typical of answers to open-ended questions in a questionnaire, then a frequency-based approach can be adopted. This often involves counting the frequency of words or synonyms.

For longer pieces of text, **qualitative content analysis** should be used. This can be conceptualised in three stages:

- **Primary analysis:** informal notes made when reading transcripts, similar to the process of **critical reading** – see Seyler (2014: Chapter 1)
- **Category formation:** this is a more formal process involving identifying types of information in transcripts, known as **categories**, and giving them a name. Categories may then be combined together into **themes**. In order for the research to be inductive, the names of the categories and themes should be new and therefore different from the concepts identified in your literature review and conceptual framework.
- **Theory generation** and **comparative analysis:** This is an optional final stage in which a theory is generated which explains how a phenomenon works across different people or situations.

For a general introduction to qualitative data analysis, please refer to Saunders et al. (2023: 664–702) and Woods (2013).

Ideally, qualitative analysis should be undertaken from a **theoretical perspective**, such as **grounded theory** (Birks and Mills, 2015). For general information on theory-based qualitative data analysis, see Schutt (2012).

Example

David provides a brief explanation of his proposed qualitative data analysis method:

> The qualitative data will be analyzed through thematic analysis in revealing the patterns and themes. Quantitative data will be subjected to descriptive statistics to get mean, frequency and percentage. Besides, the analysis of the quantitative data gathered will be coded and analyzed with the aid of NVIVO and SPSS version 16 data analysis software.

Thematic analysis is a broad term for a group of qualitative analysis techniques. David would need to refine his plan by giving a more specific choice, a citation and a rationale for it. There seems to be some confusion in his third sentence as he appears to be referring to textual data. Numerical and categorical data is not coded – this only applies to textual data. NVivo is a tool for analysing textual data (see https://lumivero.com/products/nvivo/). SPSS can also be used in textual data analysis, but its main use is with numerical and categorical data (see https://www.ibm.com/spss). Rather than briefly mentioning data analysis software tools, it would have been a better idea if David had provided more specific information about the form of data analysis he was planning to undertake, in a similar way to Dominique's paragraph above.

Ethics

You might also wish to discuss ethical issues towards the end of your methodology/methods section. These include:

- Selection from an appropriate population, such as a subsection of adults in a particular geographical area who are not deemed vulnerable
- Measures to protect participants and researchers from potential harm, such as safety in a physical data collection venue
- The right of participants to withdraw
- Collection of appropriate data, such as avoiding questions which may cause distress
- Measures to protect the identity of participants, such as anonymisation
- Protection of stored data, such as the use of password protection, encryption and secure online storage

For more information, see Oliver (2010).

Example

Lee provides a three-paragraph section on ethics. In his middle paragraph, he covers the issue of anonymisation:

> TFW are a medium sized company and previous experience has shown that it doesn't take long for information to spread throughout the company. This is

relevant as any participants in the research will be known and therefore their anonymity cannot be guaranteed. The researcher will have to ensure that if there are views or opinions expressed that these remain anonymous. This can be potentially be done by utilising strong academic writing style and this will require considerable thought when moving forward with the work. It should be acknowledged that this can be for both the researcher and participants as voicing their opinions in the public domain can also have consequences. Utilising strong academic writing should overcome this issue as having a logical progression of ideas and a strong argument should lead the reader to the same conclusion as the researcher has drawn.

It might have been better if Lee had been more explicit about his plans to ensure anonymisation, rather than stating his use of "strong academic writing." Perhaps he is referring to the use of third person language. He could have also mentioned how he would attribute the expressed opinions to individuals during data collection, such as by assigning each respondent a code. Identity protection is more than anonymity – it also relates to other textual data which might cause an individual to be identified. Lee could also have considered this.

Limitations

You might also wish to discuss potential limitations to your research at the end of this section, such as non-random sample selection in a survey, or low response rates from an online questionnaire, or potential difficulties in organising interviews or focus groups. With potential limitations, you might also discuss contingency plans you could adopt to ensure you obtain a sufficient amount of data.

Common mistakes

Here are some common mistakes that students make in writing a methodology/method section:

- Focusing too much on what different stages and choices of methodology/method mean rather than focusing on your choices and your reasons for them. There is no need to try to educate your readers about things they already understand.
- Misusing the generic descriptors quantitative and qualitative to refer to your research in general, vague terms. It is probably better to avoid these descriptors in this section, or only use them very sparingly.
- **Only explaining your choices rather than the reasons for them or how they are going to be implemented**. For example, with a choice of a questionnaire, it is important to know **why** this data collection method has been preferred to others, **how** the question design will relate to the findings of the literature review, **what** the population and sampling approach will be and **what** format it will take (e.g. paper-based or online).
- **Over-structuring your section**. For example, explaining your choice of **research design** often overlaps with other methodology subsections introduced above and is not recommended.
- **Making inconsistent choices**, such as an inductive approach and a closed form of data collection.

78 Writing the rest of your proposal

- **Only citing a single reference**, such as (Saunders et al., 2023). You need to read about methodology and method more widely and cite several authors, such as some of those recommended in this chapter.
- **Including too much critical discussion**. Your focus should be on presenting your plan for data collection and analysis within your methodological context.

Evaluating methodology/methods sections: DECJAD

The mnemonic **DECJAD** stands for:

- **D**escribe – does the subsection explain what the subsection means?
- **E**vidence – does the subsection contain evidence to back up the claims made?
- **C**hoice – does the subsection clearly explain the choices made?
- **J**ustify – are the choices justified with a persuasive argument?
- **A**pply – are the choices made applied to the context?
- **D**iscuss – does the subsection include some limited discussion towards the end?

You should not expect a yes answer for each question for each subsection as the choice of writing will be selective. However, DECJAD can help you to understand and evaluate what kinds of writing each subsection contains. The most important aspects are the four in the middle: your **choice**, your **justification** for it, supporting this with **evidence** and **applying** it to your context.

Example

Lee's methodology/methods section is evaluated in Table 12.1.

Several paragraphs from Lee's methodology/method section have already been used above as examples. The methodological aspects of his section seem to be clearer than the method aspects.

His methodological choices are clearly stated and justified with an evidence-based argument, and most of them are also applied to his context. There is a concern that his approach may be inconsistent with his philosophical choice. He also includes some discussion about the use of action research in his context. This is fine as it demonstrates his deeper thinking around his methodology and does not unbalance his section. Overall, Lee's methodology aspects are well written as he focuses on the middle four areas of the DECJAD acronym, covering each part of methodology in turn.

Lee then provides a long subsection on data collection and analysis, but it is unclear what kind of data he is planning to collect or how he is planning to analyse it. Whilst

Table 12.1 Evaluation of Lee's methodology/methods section

Subsection	Describe	Evidence	Choice	Justify	Apply	Discuss
Philosophy	✗	✓	✓	✗	✓	✗
Approach	✗	✓	✓	✓	✓	✗
Strategy	✗	✓	✓	✓	✓	✓
Data collection	✗	✓	✗	✗	✓	✗
Data analysis	✗	✗	✗	✗	✗	✗

there is some value in his explanation of how he is planning to conduct his research, it is difficult for the reader to assess the value of his method without knowing more about the data itself. Unless your choices of data collection and analysis are clear, you will devalue the utility of your methods argument.

Exercise

Evaluate the subsections of your draft methodology and methods using the DECJAD checklist given in Table 12.2.

Reflect on your evaluation of your draft section in the light of Lee's example above so that you have an idea of how to improve it.

Table 12.2 DECJAD checklist

Subsection	Describe	Evidence	Choice	Justify	Apply	Discuss
Philosophy						
Approach						
Strategy						
Data collection						
Data analysis						

Summary

This is the longest chapter in my book, indicating that writing a good methodology and method section is a difficult and complex task. Your methodology and method section provides a **plan** for your research. It has its **own vocabulary** which you will need to master. In this chapter, I recommend a structure for this section of your proposal based on presenting subsections in a logical order moving from methodology to method. With each subsection, you should focus on your **choices** and your **justification** for them, as emphasised in the DECJAD checklist above. Your language style needs to be cautious but also specific so that your reader can see that you are formulating a credible plan, but you also remain open to future changes.

References

Birks, M. and Mills, J. (2015). *Grounded Theory: A practical guide*. 2nd edn. London: SAGE.
Brace, I. and Bolton, K. (2022). *Questionnaire Design: How to plan, structure and write survey material for effective market research*. 5th edn. London: Kogan Page.
Coleman, R. (2019). *Designing Experiments for the Social Sciences: How to plan, create, and execute research using experiments*. London: SAGE.
Gobo, G. (2017). *Doing Ethnography*. 2nd edn. London: SAGE.
Hemingway, P. and Brereton, N. (2009) *What Is a Systematic Review?* 2nd edn. What is …? series (NPR09/1111). *Hayward Medical Communications*, 2, pp. 1–8.
Katz-Buonincontro, J. (2022). *How to Interview and Conduct Focus Groups*. Washington: American Psychological Association.
McNiff, J. (2013). *Action Research: Principles and practice*. 3rd edn. London: Routledge.
Oliver, P. (2010). *The Student's Guide to Research Ethics*. 2nd edn. Maidenhead: Open University Press.
Samuels, P. C. (2020). *A really simple guide to quantitative data analysis*. Technical Report. *ResearchGate*. Available at: https://doi.org/10.13140/RG.2.2.25915.36645

Saunders, M., Lewis, P. and Thornhill, A. (2023). *Research Methods for Business Students*. 9th edn. Harlow: Pearson.

Schutt, R. K. (2012). Qualitative data analysis. In R. K. Schutt, ed. *Investigating the Social World*. 7th edn. London: SAGE. [pdf] Available at: https://www.sagepub.com/sites/default/files/upmbinaries/43454_10.pdf

Seyler, D. (2014). *Read, Reason, Write: An argument text and reader*. 11th edn. New York: McGraw-Hill Education.

Woods, P. (2013). Qualitative Research. Open Educational Research Assets, The Open University. [pdf] Available at: https://www.open.edu/openlearncreate/mod/resource/view.php?id=51903

Woodside, A. G. (2010). *Case Study Research: Theory, methods and practice*. Bingley: Emerald.

13 Producing a schedule and a budget

Gantt charts

A final common section in the main body of a proposal is a schedule of tasks. The recommended way of representing this is with a **Gantt chart**. This has one row for each task and the period for doing the research project is split up equally into columns. The time span over which each task is active is then shown by filled cells in their respective row.

Research phases

As already mentioned in Chapter 1, in addition to providing tasks, it might also be useful to add **research phases** to your chart. A common characterisation of these is:

- **Conceptual** – coming up with an initial idea, formulating it and writing a proposal – this might be left out from a Gantt chart if you are submitting it with your proposal as it will already have been completed
- **Critical** – carrying out your main literature review, writing your methodology chapter, obtaining ethics approval and designing your data collection instrument
- **Action** – collecting your data and preparing it for analysis
- **Analysis** – analysing your data and writing up your findings
- **Creative** – writing your discussion and conclusions and putting your final report together

See Polit and Beck (2020).

Example

An example Gantt chart is shown in Figure 13.1.
   Some points to note about this example Gantt chart are:

- There is a **manageable number of tasks** which split the research project up in sufficient detail. It is recommended that you have between 10 and 20 tasks.
- Each task is **output orientated** – you can tell when it is complete as it relates to a specific output.
- There are a **manageable number of columns**. This example is for a part-time doctorate and uses 22 two-month columns. You should aim for between 12 and 25 columns.
- Several tasks are being conducted in **parallel** at different times.

82 Writing the rest of your proposal

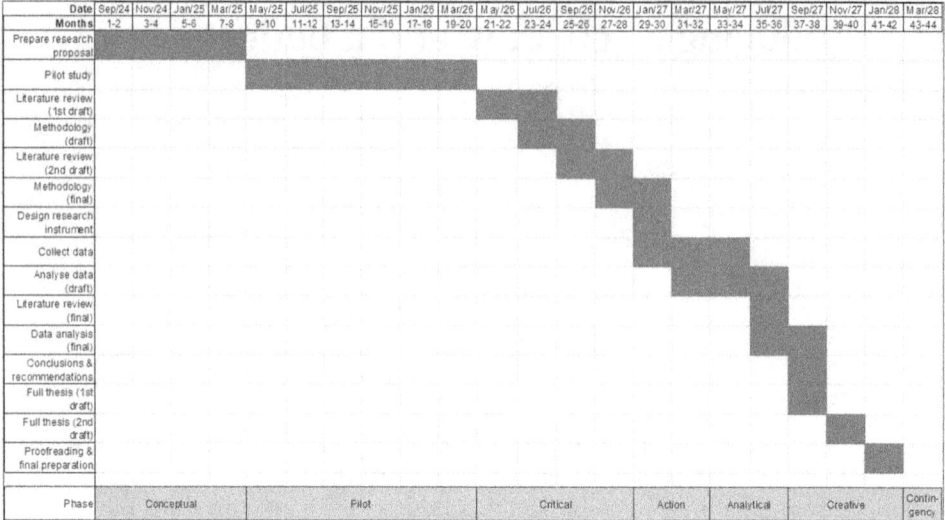

Figure 13.1 Example Gantt chart

- There are **dependencies** between some of the tasks; for example, the data in the main study cannot be analysed until data collection has started, and this cannot start until the research instrument has been designed and the ethics request has been approved. This is represented through the **research phases** at the bottom of the chart.
- There is a two-month **contingency** at the end in case there is a delay in the completion of some of the tasks.

I recommend that you use a simple spreadsheet package, such as Excel, to create your Gantt chart rather than a more sophisticated project management package. All you need to do is colour the cells relating to the time periods over which the tasks are scheduled to be active.

Example

David has provided a Gantt chart for his proposed doctoral study as shown in Figure 13.2.

David's chart is presented in portrait view using three time periods and a key. It would have been better if he had rotated the page and presented it in a single time period and added his key separately. The formatting of his chart could also be improved by making the width of each column consistent.

The number of columns on David's chart and his choice of tasks are appropriate. Also, the proposed length of the tasks appears fairly sensible. David has included phases in his research project, which is useful. However, he appears to have a misunderstanding about the meaning of the critical phase. It appears he is using this word to describe his main research project as being important rather than referring to the phase associated with his literature review and developing his methodology and method.

Producing a schedule and a budget

Date	Oct/19	Dec/19	Feb/20	Apr/20	Jun/20	Aug/20	Oct/20	Dec/20
Month	1-2	3-4	5-6	7-8	9-10	11-12	13-14	15-16
Prepare a research proposal	▓	▓						
Synopsis +paper submission			▓					
Design research instrument				▓				
Pilot study					▓			
Data collection						▓	▓	▓
Synopsis/2nd paper submission								▓
Phase	Conceptual			Critical		Action		Analytical

Date	Feb/21	Apr/21	Jun/21	Aug/21	Oct/21	Dec/21	Feb/22	Apr/22
Month	17-18	18-19	20-21	22-23	24-25	26-27	28-29	30-31
Analyse (draft)	▓							
Data analysis (final)		▓						
Literature review (1st draft)			▓					
Synopsis/ 3rd paper submission				▓				
Methodology (draft)					▓			
Literature review (final)						▓		
Methodology (final)								▓
Conclusion & recommendations								
Phase				Critical				

Date	June/22	Aug/22	Oct/22	Key & important notes:		
Month	32-33	34-35	36	-Contingency time is left to allow adjustments		
Full thesis (1st draft)	▓			-The two months interval helps to give enough room for accomplishment of tasks		
Full thesis (2nd draft)		▓		-Critical phases: shows the phases that will need more of reading and discussions		
Proofreading and final preparation				-Analytical phases: needs more analysis which may involve the use of software/new technology		
Phase	Critical		Contingency			

Figure 13.2 David's Gantt chart

Accompanying narrative

In addition to providing a Gantt chart, you should write a short narrative explaining your chart. This can describe your tasks, explain why they are in the sequence and of the length shown and then discuss possible issues relating to managing your research project.

Providing a budget

You may be required to provide a budget of associated expenses as part of your proposal. The approval of your proposal might then also mean the approval of the associated budget. Expenses should be identified in different categories. There should be justification for them and also an explanation of how they have been calculated. The budget you present should be clear and reasonable, based on a common sense understanding of the

84 Writing the rest of your proposal

costs involved in undertaking your research project. You should neither under-estimate nor over-estimate your costs. However, it might be important to understand how costs are established in your institution, such as the use of an approved agent for organising transport.

Example

Esther has provided a budget for her proposed research project as shown in Figure 13.3.

Esther's budget is itemised, but the meaning of some of her proposed expenses is unclear. Also, she has not provided an associated narrative to justify or explain her costs. It is therefore unlikely that her proposal would be approved with this budget included within it as it is unlikely that the committee making the decision would be willing to release these funds without knowing more about how she was planning to spend them and why they were necessary.

Proposed Budget

ITEM	COST
Travel Costs	1,000,000
Data Costs	1,000,000
Material Costs	1,000,000
Prototyping Costs	2,000,000
Testing Costs	2,000,000
Production Costs	3,000,000
Assistants Costs	1,000,000
Time Costs	1,000,000
Exhibition Costs	1,000,000
Total	13,000,000

Figure 13.3 Esther's proposed budget

Exercise

Use a spreadsheet package to create a draft Gantt chart like the example above that represents the tasks and phases in your research project, then draft an accompanying narrative that explains it and discusses potential problems that you might encounter and how you plan to manage them.

Summary

A schedule and a budget are important practical aspects of a research project. You should present clear information along with a simple justification which can be understood by non-specialist readers. Try to use common sense and think practically and realistically about what you will need to do, how long it might take and how much it might cost. The tasks in a doctorate can be thought of in terms of research phases. You need to consider the critical dependencies between some tasks.

Reference

Polit, D. and Beck, C. (2020). *Essentials of Nursing Research: Appraising evidence for nursing practice*. 10th edn. Amber, PA: Lippincott Williams & Wilkins.

14 Referencing

Introduction

Referencing is the systematic process of attributing external sources and presented data (tables and charts) within your proposal. Attributing external sources commonly involves **citing** in the main body of the text followed by a reference in a list at the end. In social sciences, this often means using an **alphabetical style** referencing system, such as Harvard or APA. This means the references in the list should be given in the alphabetical order of the author(s) or institutions who created them.

You should be given specific guidance on how to reference at your institution. For general principles on referencing, please refer to Pears and Shields (2022) and its associated website (https://www.citethemrightonline.com/). For additional guidance on some common referencing systems, please refer to the referencing resources in the Purdue Online Writing Lab (https://owl.purdue.edu/owl/research_and_citation/resources.html).

Please also refer to Chapter 6 for additional guidance on using evidence. The focus of this chapter is on using referencing systems correctly, but obviously, this will depend on the referencing system you are using.

Citing

With alphabetical referencing systems, the author's surname is used in the citation. This can be done at the end of a sentence by putting the name and the year of the publication in a bracket, which is known as an **indirect citation**. Alternatively, the author's name can be put in a sentence and just the year is put in a bracket, which is known as a **direct citation**. Generally, when using an alphabetical referencing system, direct citations are preferred as they make the writing appear more personal and allow you to provide a richer citation. However, a downside is that they use more words.

There are also rules about sources with **multiple authors**, which depend on the system being used, and how to present **quotations** (word-for-word citations).

Examples

David begins his background with the following extract from his first paragraph:

> At the beginning of the 21st century, Phillipson (1992) and Brock-Utne et al., (2010) indicate that either teachers or learners were challenged by integrating the content and

the English language of instruction in the teaching and learning process. On the side of learners, Brock-Utne et al. (2010) state that, the content and language integrated program was introduced with the main purpose to improve language skills, especially in reading and listening. Later, this program was found (Pang, 2018; Pflepsen, 2015) inadequate to solve the indicated problem. It was criticized that it mainly focused on the basic interpersonal communicational skills in learning science (Clegg& Simpson, 2016).

We may observe the following about David's citation style:

- He is using both direct citations and indirect citations.
- There are two direct citations in his first sentence (Phillipson (1992) and Brock-Utne et al., *(2010)*). He has done this correctly for the APA style which he is required to use.
- These direct citations are connected to the sentence by a **reporting verb** (*indicate*). Reporting verbs enable you to create brief summaries of cited literature.
- *Et al.* stands for "and others." It is a standard abbreviation in many referencing systems and is used when a reference has multiple authors.
- Perhaps the indirect style would have been better here as David seems to be placing too much emphasis on researchers rather than factual information at the beginning of his proposal.
- It is also advisable to try to avoid repeating citations in the same paragraph. David has re-used *Brock-Utne et al. (2010)* later on. Perhaps this could have been rewritten somehow?
- David also uses indirect citations later on (*(Pang, 2018; Pflepsen, 2015)*). This has also been done correctly. The correct way to separate two indirect citations in the APA style is to use a semicolon (;).
- However, it is unusual to put indirect citations in the middle of a sentence. It would have been more conventional to place these at the end of this sentence.
- He has another indirect citation at the end of the next sentence (*(Clegg& Simpson, 2016)*). This is also a correct use of the APA style apart from the missing space after *Clegg*.
- Overall David has demonstrated a good use of both direct and indirect citations in this paragraph extract.

Lee provides a **direct quote** with an indirect citation in his methodology:

The proposed research philosophy for undertaking this work is a Positivist approach. The ontological position of positivism is one of realism. 'The positivist epistemology is one of objectivism. Positivists go forth into the world impartially, discovering absolute knowledge about an objective reality' (Scotland, 2012:10).

Lee is using a version of the Harvard referencing system. His indirect citation is correct apart from a missing space between "*2012:*" and the page number "*10*," and he should have used double quotation marks instead of single ones. In most referencing systems, direct quotes should always have page numbers when the cited source has numbered pages. Page numbers are optional with other forms of citation. However, rather than presenting his quote without any forewarning, a direct style might have worked better here, such as:

According to Scotland (2012: 10), "The positivist epistemology is one of…"

Tables and figures

Tables and figures should be labelled consistently. With most referencing systems, they should referred to in the text **before** they are presented. If they contain data from an external source, this should be acknowledged including the page number, where it exists.

Examples

Esther provides an image of an ancient leather shoe in her literature review which she has labelled as follows:

> Figure 2: Chalcolithic leather shoe from Areni 1 cave; ca 5000 BCE. Source Wikipedia

- Esther has correctly added a number to her figure and provided a caption which explains the figure.
- Esther has placed her caption below her figure. This is the wrong place with the APA referencing style. It should be placed above the figure and the figure number and the caption should be on separate lines – see https://apastyle.apa.org/style-grammar-guidelines/tables-figures/figures. Only the citation should be placed below the figure in a note.
- She has also not referred to Figure 2 in her text preceding her presentation of this figure.
- Also, it is not acceptable to just cite the source of her image as Wikipedia. However, Wikipedia cites many acceptable academic sources. By entering Esther's caption title into Google, I was able to establish that her image appears to be taken from Pinhasi et al. (2010).

Lee provides a table in his introduction with the following caption:

Table 1. The UK is the 9th Largest Manufacturer in the world by output. Source: House of Commons Library (2018)

We may observe the following:

- Lee has provided a caption which includes the table number.
- He has placed the label before the table, which is the correct order with the Harvard referencing system.
- He has also cited this table in his proposal text before he presented it, which is also correct.
- He has also added a source citation. However, when using the Harvard referencing system, the institutional author should go in the bracket, i.e. *(House of Commons Library, 2018)*. Also, as explained below, it turns out that this publication was created by Chris Rhodes. Individual authors should generally be cited where they are available. I was also able to find the table he had reproduced and the page number on which it appeared in the original document (4).

- The only other problem is Lee's caption content – it is an interpretation of the relevance of the table to his context rather than a description of the table itself. He should have left the interpretation for the argument in his text.

His caption should therefore have been written something like:

Table 1. Manufacturing output of the 20 largest national economies in 2015. Source: (Rhodes, 2018: 4).

Reference lists

With in-text citation styles of referencing, a reference list should be provided at the end of the proposal which includes all the sources cited in the text. With alphabetical in-text style systems, these should be presented in the alphabetical order of the first author. Only one reference should be provided for each source even if it has been cited several times. The sources should not be split up according to the type of publication.

Each type of citation (for example, journal articles, books and electronic reports) has a different citation style, but they have common features. You should not simply cut and paste citations of your cited sources from someone else's work as these may not conform to your institution's style. However, you can use these as the basis for creating your own references. Google Scholar (https://scholar.google.co.uk/) also has a 99 *Cite* link which you can use to obtain citation details in standard formats.

Examples

David's reference corresponding to his citation of (Pflepsen, 2015) is:

> Pflepsen, A. (2015). Planning for Language Use in Education: Best Practices and Practical Steps to Improve Learning Outcomes. NC: RTI International.

This document appears to be an organisational report. In order to double-check his citation, I put the author's surname, the year of publication and the first part of the source title into Google Scholar. This yielded a single document as shown in Figure 14.1.

The APA style citation provided by the 99 *Cite* link in Google Scholar was:

> Pflepsen, A., Benson, C., Chabbott, C., & van Ginkel, A. (2015). *Planning for language use in education: Best practices and practical steps to improve learning outcomes.* USAID Bureau for Africa. https://www.researchgate.net/publication/281823056_Planning_for_Language_Use_in_Education_Best_Practices_and_Practical_Steps_to_Improve_Learning_Outcomes. Accessed March, 8, 2016.

Clicking on the link to the document, it was clear that the other authors included in the Google Scholar reference had also made contributions to producing the document, so it seemed to be appropriate that they should have been included. It was also clear from this document that all the authors worked for an organisation called *RTI International* which prepared the document, but it was prepared for *USAID Bureau for Africa* and produced

90   *Writing the rest of your proposal*

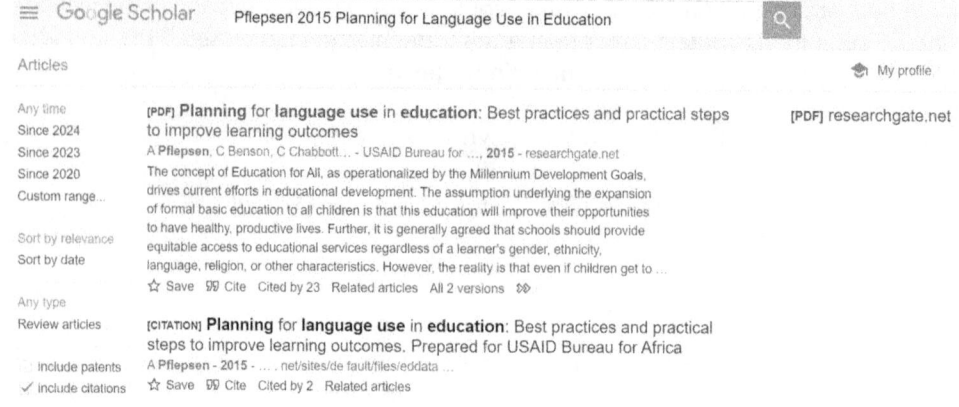

Figure 14.1 Output of Google Scholar search

by *USAID*. Therefore, either *USAID Bureau for Africa* or *USAID* are probably better names for the publishing organisation in the reference.

There is no need to specify the place of publication with a report in APA style. The URL in the Google Scholar reference is inappropriate as it is not the formal publication site of the document. I put the full title and the publisher's name into Google and the first result was a more official publication site, as shown in Figure 14.2.

By right-clicking on the hyperlink in this result, I was able to obtain an official URL for this document: https://pdf.usaid.gov/pdf_docs/pbaaf479.pdf. As David is using

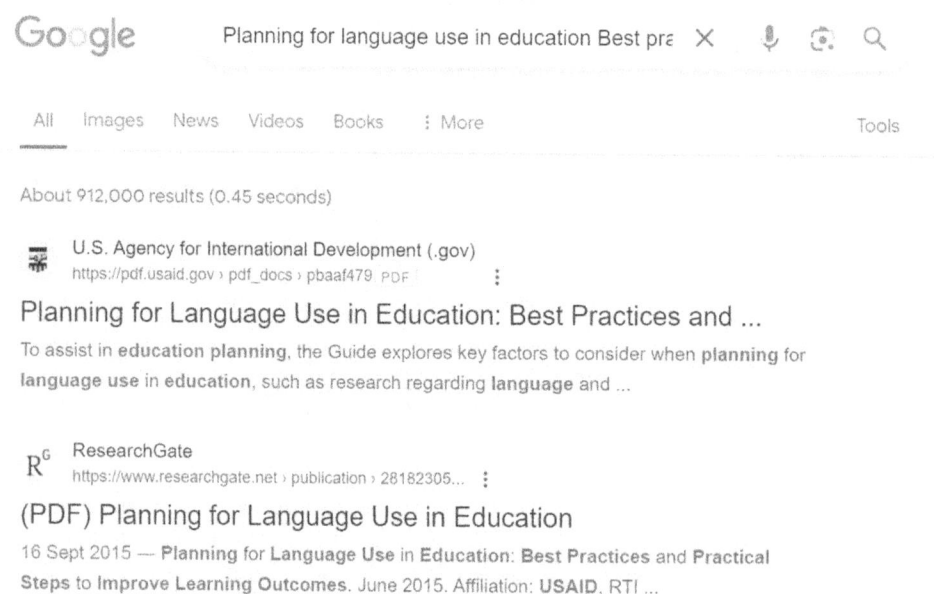

Figure 14.2 Output of the Google search

APA style, there is no need to provide an accessed date. This yields the overall reference as:

Pflepsen, A., Benson, C., Chabbott, C., & van Ginkel, A. (2015). *Planning for language use in education: Best practices and practical steps to improve learning outcomes*. USAID Bureau for Africa. **https://pdf.usaid.gov/pdf_docs/pbaaf479.pdf**.

Notice that the report title is in italics, not the publishing organisation. Apart from the first letter of the title and subtitle, the only letters that should be in capitals are for proper nouns or acronyms. The URL should be in bold and black text.

Lee provides a reference for his (House of Commons, 2018) citation in his institutional Harvard style as follows:

House of Commons Library. (2018) *Manufacturing International comparisons*. Available at: https://researchbriefings.files.parliament.uk/documents/SN05809/SN05809.pdf [Accessed 06 May 2019].

The link he provided is to an official website and is still working at the time of publication of this book. Having obtained the document, I was able to ascertain that it was a briefing paper written by Chris Rhodes and published by the UK Parliament which includes the House of Commons and its Library. It also had a number: 05809. By checking the Harvard referencing guide for Lee's institution, I was able to determine that the document type was a House of Commons paper which meant that the reference should have been presented as follows:

Rhodes, C. (2018) *Manufacturing: International comparisons*. (HC 05809 2017-18). Available at: https://researchbriefings.files.parliament.uk/documents/SN05809/SN05809.pdf [Accessed 6 May 2019].

HC stands for House of Commons. 2017-18 refers to the parliamentary session in which the report was published.

Summary

It is important that you know in advance what style of referencing you need to use in your proposal, and that you obtain a style guide for it. If you are required to use an alphabetical system, there are different ways to cite in your proposal, and the style of reference in your reference list will depend upon the referencing system and the type of document that you have cited. It is important to establish the correct author(s) or institutional creator of a document when you are citing. Direct quotes should include page numbers, where present.

Google Scholar can be useful for identifying documents. However, just because you are able to obtain a document online does not mean that it is just a webpage – you need to work out exactly what kind of online resource it is and then refer to a guide for referencing system you are using to work out how to write its reference.

The 99 *Cite* link in Google Scholar can be used to obtain an initial approximation to a reference in some common reference systems but you should not rely on this fully as it may be inaccurate. You should not use unofficial URLs for referencing electronic documents. Google can also be useful for obtaining the official URLs provided by the publishing organisation.

Finally, there are different ways of labelling tables and figures according to the referencing system you are using. As for online documents, you should ensure that you attribute their official sources, including a page number where present.

References

Pinhasi, R., Gasparian, B., Areshian, G., Zardaryan, D., Smith, A., Bar-Oz, G. and Higham, T. (2010). First direct evidence of chalcolithic footwear from the Near Eastern Highlands. *PloS ONE*, 5(6), e10984. https://doi.org/10.1371/journal.pone.0010984

Pears, R. and Shields, G. (2022). *Cite Them Right*. 12th edn. London: Bloomsbury Academic.

Part V
After submitting your proposal

Introduction

Now that we have covered everything involved in deciding on, researching and writing your proposal, the remainder of this book provides five chapters containing on your next steps as a doctoral research student. There are many other resources written on these subjects, which no doubt you will be accessing, but these chapters provide some initial brief guidance and pointers of where to look for more information. It is written from the perspective of a doctoral student who has just submitted their proposal.

Chapter 15 covers presenting and defending your proposal. Chapter 16 explores writing an extended proposal. Chapter 17 focuses on planning and managing your research, including stress management. Chapter 18 explores managing your relationships with your supervisors. Finally chapter 19 introduces the tasks you will be undertaking after submitting your proposal, commonly referred to as the **critical phase** of doing a doctorate (see the *Research phases* sections of Chapter 1 and Chapter 13).

15 Presenting and defending your proposal

Introduction

You may have been required to create a presentation on your proposed study earlier in your doctoral journey, such as at the interview stage. If so, then clearly parts of this could be reused and updated. In this chapter, we will focus on creating and defending a presentation which is consistent with your completed proposal.

In this chapter, we will consider how to develop a proposal presentation, a recommended structure presentation delivery and how to handle questions after delivering your presentation.

Developing a proposal presentation

If you have been asked to create a proposal presentation, then you need to clearly understand the **brief** for the presentation, the nature of your **audience** and **general principles** about developing a presentation.

Understanding your brief

You should be given a brief for your presentation which should indicate the required **content**, the **time** available and the delivery **format**. Usually the content is just about your research idea and how you plan to investigate it, but it might also contain a reflection on your development as a researcher, or your personal rationale for investigating this subject. Read your brief carefully. Ask for clarification if you are unsure about anything. It would be a big mistake to put much effort into creating a presentation which was not what was required.

Assuming you are required to present a normal style of slide presentation, use the **time limit** to estimate how many slides you should create. It is recommended that you should have **no more than one slide per minute** of your presentation. Alternatively, the **main body** of your presentation should be **about one slide every two minutes**.

In terms of the **format** of delivery, first of all, it is important to establish whether the event will be in person, online or hybrid. Will you be able to use your own laptop, or should you send your presentation as a file in advance or will you be able to upload it from a storage device, such as a flash drive? What software will be installed on the computer you will be using? What operating system will it use?

DOI: 10.4324/9781003434344-21

It is important that you know the answers to these questions in advance so that you can plan for your delivery. It will look unprofessional if your presentation delivery is hindered by a technical fault which you could have avoided through better planning. Your audience should generally be sympathetic, but if you end up wasting their time in a way which could have been avoided, then they are likely to lose some of their goodwill towards you.

Know your audience

It is important to establish what your audience already know about your subject area. Usually, this means that you should target your presentation at **non-specialists**. Therefore, you should at least make your title slide, your background, your problem statement and your front matter accessible to a general audience by avoiding jargon, technical language and non-essential abbreviations.

Other aspects which non-specialists often ask about is the **data** you propose to collect in your study and the **method** you propose to use to analyse it. These should be clearly explained and justified.

General principles about presentations

You should make your slides clear and easy to read. Use a consistent background colour, title font and main body font. I recommend that you use a **San serif font**, i.e. one which don't have additional lines at the end of their characters (Encyclopaedia Britannica, 1992), such as **Arial**. An **off-white background** colour, such as light yellow or pink, is also generally recommended from a neurodiverse perspective to avoid visual stress (Evans, 2001). You should also avoid small font sizes and any unreadable text.

It is a good idea to present a **limited amount of text** on each slide and, where appropriate, to also include a **single image** which is directly related to the text (Mayer and Moreno, 2003). Miller's (1956) *seven plus or minus two* rule is useful here – your audience will only be able to take in about seven pieces of information at once and so do not present overly complex slides. Another mistake to avoid is reading out all the text on your slides. Generally, what you say should be in more depth than the text on your slides and it should complement the textual information presented. The only exception is your front matter; this is why it is important to make sure your front matter is as clear and concise as possible.

Animations should be kept to a minimum in an academic context. Use colour, font size and font type consistently as any changes to them can have an implicit meaning. You should focus on the clarity and simplicity of your content.

Example

Figure 15.1 displays one of Lee's slides from a draft presentation he created in the process of developing his proposal. Notice how he uses a simple image to complement the text. He also uses a consistent font style and limited text. His font is San serif. Perhaps he could have also changed his background colour.

Presenting and defending your proposal 97

> # Literature Review
> - Lean
> - The Sand Cone Model
> - Other:
>   - Six Sigma
>   - TQM
>   - Business Process Re-Engineering

Figure 15.1 Literature review slide from Lee's draft proposal

Recommended structure

Here is my recommended structure for a presentation lasting about 12 minutes:

Slide 1.	Title slide
Slide 2.	Background
Slide 3.	Problem statement
Slide 4.	Aim and objectives
Slide 5.	Research questions
Slide 6.	Literature review – main thematic areas
Slide 7.	Methods
Slide 8.	Schedule
Slide 9.	References
Slide 10.	Thank you and questions

Your title slide should include your proposed research title, your name, your degree course, your institution and any other essential information relevant to the context of your presentation.

There is no need for a summary slide as your audience will understand the structure of a proposal presentation.

Your background slide should contain about three main concepts which can be combined together to establish your research topic, as already explained in Chapter 9.

Your problem statement slide should take the concepts you introduced in your background slide, combine them together and explain what is already known about this area, thus establishing your research gap, as explained in Chapter 9.

Your front matter needs to be clear, concise, consistent and use the correct genre, as explained in Chapter 3. You may need to summarise your front matter if it is too long to present it in full on your title slide and two main body slides.

Your literature review slide does not need to have a lot of details as the focus of your presentation should be on presenting your front matter based on the research gap you have established, and the methods you plan to use to investigate this topic. These should be understandable to non-specialist audience members. All you need to present are the general thematic areas you have identified and your initial insights into them (see Lee's example above).

As already mentioned, your audience is more likely to be interested in your method than your methodology, as this is something understandable to non-specialists. Assuming you are proposing to undertake a primary data collection study, you need to clearly explain what data you are planning to collect, how much of it you intend to collect and how you are planning to analyse it. This needs to make sense in terms of what is needed and what is achievable within the constraints of your proposed study. Please refer to the *Sample size recommendations for surveys* section in Chapter 12.

Your schedule should then follow on from and incorporate your data collection and analysis plan. The active phase of your research is essentially what drives your whole study. It needs to be given sufficient time and the stages which precede and follow it should enable and make use of it. It might be sufficient to present a Gantt chart here. Make sure that the tasks and the timescales are legible on your slide.

You do not need a conclusion. You do not need to present your reference list slide unless you are asked to refer to it. You can then move straight to your final slide which should thank your audience for their attention and invite them to ask questions.

Delivering your presentation

Having prepared good presentation slides does not guarantee a good delivery but it can certainly enhance the process. Other things you need to consider are:

- **Your appearance** – you should dress appropriately for the occasion. You should check your appearance in a mirror before entering the room.
- **Your posture** – if you are delivering in person, decide how you are going to stand. Try not to touch your face or head as you deliver. Put your hands behind your back if you are not comfortable giving gestures and don't know what to do with them.
- **Speech and pace** – try to speak fairly slowly and clearly, and sufficiently loudly so that everyone can hear you without straining their ears.
- **Socially connect with your audience** – it is good if you can make the audience feel comfortable at the start. Try to maintain eye contact with them as well. You might feel sufficiently confident to point to parts of your presentation to emphasise them or to move around during your delivery. Avoid reading out your own presentation, except for your front matter.
- **Technology** – you could use a clicker with a laser pointing device.
- **Prompt cards** – rather than continually turning round to your slides, you could create some prompt cards with short notes on them for each slide in the main body of your presentation.
- **Practicing** – perhaps the most important thing to do is to practise before you deliver your presentation, maybe with some of your fellow doctoral students.
- **Panic avoidance** – if you feel yourself starting to panic, take a sip of water or highlight a on the current slide in order to emphasise it and to take your attention away from yourself.

For additional guidance, please see Skidmore et al. (2010).

Handling questions after your presentation

You might be interrupted during your presentation, but this is unlikely. If it does happen, it is probably because the enquirer believes that there is some important information you have either left out or you need to clarify. Make sure you understand what they are asking and try to answer their question quickly so that you can regain your presentation flow. If there are several interruptions, you should look to the meeting chair to advocate for you as this could be unfair. They should support you to be allowed to deliver your presentation in the time available.

Here is some guidance for handling questions at the end of your presentation:

- Make sure you understand what is being asked. If it is not clear, ask them to repeat or rephrase their question.
- If you are able to answer it, stick to talking about that and try to give a concise response. Do not use this as an opportunity for a long digression about parts of your presentation which you did not have time to talk about.
- If you don't know the answer to the question, be honest, thank them for their question and admit that you don't have an answer rather than trying to make something up on the spot. You might also offer to go away and think about it then get back to them.

Summary

Creating and delivering a presentation to accompany your proposal is an important complementary skill which will provide you with experience and confidence for other presentations in the future. Proposal presentation requirements may vary, so it is important to understand what you have been asked to do. Your presentation slides should not contain too much text and might be complemented by simple images. You should focus on the essential information in your proposal and use a logical structure and the right number of slides for the time available. Practice and the principles explained above can help you to improve your presentation delivery technique.

References

Encyclopaedia Britannica (1992). *Sans serif in The New Encyclopaedia Britannica*, 15th edn. Chicago: Encyclopaedia Britannica Inc., Vol. 10, p. 421.
Evans, B. J. W. (2001). *Dyslexia and Vision*. London: Whurr.
Mayer, R. E. and Moreno, R. (2003). Nine ways to reduce cognitive load in multimedia learning. *Educational Psychologist*, 38(1), pp. 43–52.
Miller, G. A. (1956). The magical number seven, plus or minus two: some limits on our capacity for processing information. *Psychological Review*, 63(2), pp. 81–97.
Skidmore, S. T., Slate, J. R. and Onwuegbuzie, A. J. (2010). Developing effective presentation skills: evidence-based guidelines. *Research in the Schools*, 17(2), pp. 25–37.

16 Writing another proposal

Introduction

There are different reasons why you may be required to write another proposal. The two main reasons are to make changes so that it can be approved and to turn a local department or school-level proposal into one for a higher-level committee. In this chapter, we shall firstly explore addressing the feedback you receive on your first proposal. Secondly, we shall consider the requirements for a second proposal, such as the expectations and abilities of committee members. Finally, we shall look at strategies for turning a local proposal into a higher level one.

Addressing feedback on your proposal

At some point you should receive written feedback on your proposal. If this is not what you expected, you may need to give yourself space and time to get beyond your emotional reaction before engaging with the detail of the feedback. Talk over your disappointment with others and sleep on the matter.

Once you are in a more objective mindset, you should read your feedback in detail and see what you can learn about how to improve your work, your understanding of the research process and your ability as an academic writer.

The first and most important thing to focus on is to **improve your doctoral research topic**. This is your main opportunity to receive detailed feedback on your topic and to decide whether it needs changing. You should be prepared to make changes and not be wedded to your proposal idea. However, as mentioned in Chapter 2, it is much better to adapt an existing idea than start again from scratch. From my experience, most proposal topic ideas are criticised for being **too broad in scope**. Doctoral students often go through a narrowing down process in the first third of their studies. You will need to agree with your supervisor on a viable topic and then **rewrite your front matter** to make it consistent with this topic choice. Once an improvement to your research topic is established, you can assess the relevance of the rest of the feedback.

You may receive feedback that your plan for collecting and analysing data to investigate your chosen topic was not viable. Some doctoral students are too ambitious because they do not realise how much work is involved, especially in analysing qualitative data.

The other advice you have received in your feedback can help you with drafting the first three chapters of your thesis: your introduction, your literature review and your methodology. Make use of this good opportunity to improve as a writer.

Understanding the requirements for another proposal

If you are rewriting your proposal for the same process, then you should simply follow the original brief you were given along with your feedback. Make sure that it is written for the correct audience.

If your original proposal was approved and you are now turning it into a new document you need to consider what are the requirements for this audience, their characteristics and the function of this new document.

In my voluntary work in East Africa, I am continually surprised how the vast proportion of doctoral students do not know why they are writing a proposal or who it is for. You need to think about your main audience being the decision-makers on your new document. Relevant questions are:

- How much do they know about your research area?
- How experienced are they?
- How busy are they? How long might they spend reading your new document?
- What are the expectations at your institution for a revised proposal?

The answer to the first question will probably be that they are less knowledgeable about your research area than the committee members for your first submission. This means that you should make your document **accessible** to them by avoiding jargon, technical language or using too many acronyms.

They are likely to be more experienced than the first submission committee. This means that they may be more vocal and critical about some of the details of your content. They may also have certain beliefs and biases based on their personal and disciplinary perspectives. Therefore, it will be important for you to re-read your proposal and consider the strength and quality of your argument.

The final two questions may lead to a dilemma: firstly, the members of this higher committee are likely to be even busier than the people who made the decision on your original proposal. This means that they will have even less time to form an opinion on it. Secondly, there may be some institutional expectation that you write a longer document. Some institutions expect their doctoral students to be working towards the first three chapters of their thesis by the time that they submit their revised proposal to a higher committee. Long documents and busy committee members who are senior researchers are potentially a really bad combination. This may be the challenge that you will need to negotiate.

In view of this, the most important thing to do is to ensure that your **argument is clear**. Remembering the bear and the fish metaphor from the front cover and the section on what your reader is looking for in the Introduction chapter; you should ensure that the most important aspects of your proposal, such as your **front matter**, are easy to find, clear, use the correct genre and are consistent. It should also be straightforward to follow the **rationale** for your choice of topic in your introduction. In your **literature review**, you should ensure that there is a logical structure and that each subsection is brought to a clear conclusion. The end of your literature review should focus on your topic and reappraise your aim or research questions in the light of your preliminary findings. The structure of your **methodology/ method** section also needs to be logical, and your decisions need to be clearly presented with a justification.

Turning your initial proposal into an extended one

An extended proposal is likely to have a longer introduction, literature review and methodology/method. Please refer to Chapter 19 for advice on writing extended literature reviews and methodology chapters.

Rewriting your introduction

In terms of writing an extended introduction, do not add unnecessary background or many additional subsections to it as this will not improve your document. Remember that the purpose of an introduction is to introduce your chosen topic. The purpose of your background is therefore to provide the **necessary context** for introducing your topic. This does not mean that it has to be the same length – you can still make it longer, but you need to be clear about the purpose of any descriptive information that you present here.

Your problem statement can be longer, but again it should form a bridge between the discrete conceptual areas you have introduced in your background and your aim. You might combine the concepts in your background together more slowly and you may spend longer presenting similar research to your own proposed topic in order to justify your research gap.

It is advisable not to make your front matter any longer in a revised proposal. I have already covered revising your topic idea and rewriting your associated front matter earlier in this chapter.

As explained in Chapter 9, additional subsections of an introduction you might include are a rationale, a thesis statement, the scope or location of your study, potential limitations, significance or potential impact and an outline of the rest of your proposal. Based on what you provided in your original proposal, I advise that you do not add all of these but begin by considering adding which of them might **improve your proposal the most** and **only add one**.

Revising your schedule and budget

You may have received feedback on your schedule or your budget from your initial proposal submission. You will probably need to change your timeline in your schedule a little because of the later submission date for another proposal. There is no particular need to provide more detailed information here unless it has been requested. Please refer to Chapter 13 for advice on writing these sections.

Summary

In this chapter, we have considered two main contexts for writing another proposal – a resubmission and a longer proposal for a higher-level committee. With both contexts, the first thing to establish is whether any changes are needed to your topic idea. Otherwise, when resubmitting a proposal, you should be given feedback which you need to follow.

If you are writing a longer proposal for another committee, then you should understand the psychology of your target readers. A longer proposal does not mean it is better. You need to focus on maintaining a logical structure in your document with a clear argument.

17 Planning and managing your research

Time management

General principles

Here are some general time management tips, some of which are based on the advice available from Coaching Positive Performance (2018):

- Try to address and **resolve any emotional or social distractions** before you try to start working as these can affect your ability to concentrate. You will need to spend some time investing in developing effective working relationships with those around you.
- Use critical thinking to **identify and evaluate** the **tasks** you need to complete: write them down and assess their relative levels of **urgency** and **importance**. For example, you could write them on post-it notes and place them on a grid – see Figure 17.1. Make sure you leave enough time for important tasks which are less urgent (priority 2) as these can often bite you if you focus too much on urgent tasks which are less important (priority 3).
- Based on your task list and evaluation, **choose the right task to do first** then **focus** on it: you will have a better overall outcome if you focus on and spend enough time doing high priority tasks well.

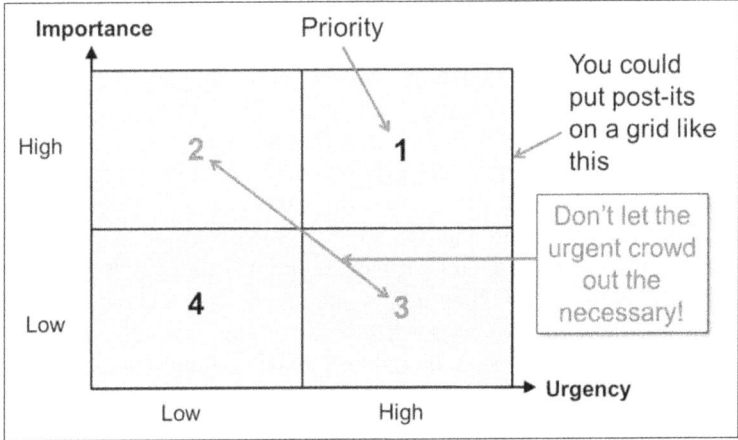

Figure 17.1 Task ranking by urgency and importance

DOI: 10.4324/9781003434344-23

- It is good to be aware of your own self-motivation and use this to improve your performance. For example, do you enjoy finishing tasks? Do you like to keep your information tidy? Would a picture help you to get your thoughts down on paper before focusing on a writing task? What is your next social commitment relating to your research project and how do you need to prepare for it?
- Doing a doctorate requires **discipline**. You may need to be a little ruthless and forego some of your other interests and responsibilities for a period of time and learn to say 'no' to some new demands on your time. Do you really need to be doing them now? Can someone else handle them?
- However, you still need to have a life outside of your doctorate. Make sure you **get sufficient rest**, **eat well** and **don't withdraw socially**. You will perform better overall if you don't overdo things as you can easily wear yourself out.
- Try to maintain **accurate, organised records**, as these can help you when you need to refer back to what you have already done. One strategy is to keep a **research log** – a general book of notes covering your research project.

Getting started

One major challenge you may face is **how to get started** on a big new task, such as those covered in Chapter 19. Here are some tips for getting started and improving your productivity based on McMillan and Weyers (2011):

- Think about your **study environment**: Is it tidy? Is it too noisy? Could you change location and work more productively?
- Try to **avoid social distractions** – find a place and time where you can concentrate. This might mean switching off social media or your email inbox for a while.
- Work in **short bursts** rather than pressuring yourself to achieve too much over a longer period.
- **Find a way to start**, even if it is not the task at the top of your list, do something relating to your research project that you feel comfortable with. Reject **displacement activities** – unrelated tasks which suddenly seem important because you are trying to face something difficult.
- Focus on **positives**, such as what you have already achieved, rather than what you haven't yet accomplished.
- Use a **non-linear approach to writing**: you can outline or draft some chapters whilst you refine others. You cannot hope to complete your chapters in linear order before starting the next one as you will surely run out of time.
- **Break down large tasks**: whilst Gantt charts are good for seeing the big picture, they lack the detail required to manage larger tasks. One way of managing this is through a **work breakdown structure**, such as the example shown in Table 17.1.
- **Work alongside others**: whilst doctoral research work is largely individual, there are ways that you can take advantage of other people's activities, such as your university friends or other people studying a research project. If you were to go to a study location together and take breaks at the same time, you could **set goals** and report back on your progress.
- **Ask for help**: if you get stuck, don't suffer on your own, but speak out to someone about it, such as your supervisors, a fellow student, or your doctoral course director. You can waste a lot of time and heartache by keeping quiet when someone else might be able to assist you or at least point you in the right direction to find help.

Table 17.1 Example work breakdown structure

Task no.	Description	Effort	Who	Resources/comment
3.1	Develop pilot interview questions	6 hrs	Me	
3.2	Supervisor to check questionnaire	1 hr	Supervisor	Arrange meeting for 20th Feb
3.3	Arrange 3 interviews	2 hrs	Me	
3.4	Carry out 3 interviews	10 hrs	Me	Arrange payment
3.5	Analyse interview data	10 hrs	Me	Make comments in reflective journal
3.6	Send improved interview questions to supervisor	2 hrs	Me	

- **Don't be a perfectionist**: some students find it hard to let go of their draft work because they are worried that it is not good enough and their supervisors might criticise them. It is your supervisors' job to give you feedback on your draft work and this is perhaps the most important thing that they do. They are not trying to criticise you – they are trying to help you to improve your work and also to develop as a researcher and as an academic writer. This means that you need to have the courage to trust them with your draft work at the right moment. If you leave it too, late you will not have enough time to make changes and you might already think your work is better than it actually is.

Finishing on time

According to Horn (2012), these are some common causes of delay in research projects:

- Problems accessing data or participants
- Illness
- Unavailability of resources
- Slow ethics approval, especially if your topic has been viewed as medium or high risk
- A difficult academic area – maybe the area you have chosen is relatively new and appropriate methods for undertaking research are not yet agreed
- A family or work crisis
- Delays in receiving feedback from your supervisors, or their feedback unexpectedly requires you to rewrite chapters or sections

The moral of all these common causes of delay is to **leave some contingency time** in your schedule. Failure to do so will make you feel stressed and mean that you will not do yourself justice as you will not be able to finish all the tasks involved in completing your thesis to an adequate standard.

Here is some advice from some successful medical students (Rivera et al., 2005) on how to complete a scholarly research project on time:

- Start early
- Set aside adequate (protected) time each week
- Stick to your timeline
- Get the most out of your supervisory relationship
- Choose a topic that genuinely interests you
- Keep your project simple yet innovative

Stress management

Definition

Emotional, or human, stress is a concept derived from the physical concept of stress. In the physical context, **strain** means the amount of tension that an object is placed under. **Stress** is the amount of reaction of that object to being placed under strain.

According to Lazarus and Cohen (1977), **emotional stress** occurs when you believe you cannot cope with a problem or situation you perceive to be stressful.

Causes

According to Fontana (1993), there are a number of possible causes of stress relating to doctoral studies:

- Insufficient support or leadership
- Long or unsociable hours
- Uncertainty or insecurity
- Unrealistically high expectations
- Inability to influence decisions (caused by a lack of assertiveness)
- Conflicts with your supervisors
- Poor communication
- Inability to finish a job

Stress and productivity

Doctoral students often feel stressed because they are **putting themselves under too much strain** as they are trying to achieve too much in the time they have allocated. With better planning and lower expectations of what you are trying to achieve over a period of time, you can actually achieve more, especially in the long run.

If you feel you are working near your limit, you need to **be kind to yourself**, **pull back** and **get some rest**. You cannot maintain maximum productivity over an extended period as your productivity will start to drop off. Once you get into a mindset of trying too hard, you can do yourself physical harm such as exhaustion, ill health or even a breakdown, as well as not achieving as much.

Signs

Here are some possible signs of stress:

- Panic attacks
- Always feeling pressured and hurried
- Unable to take in new information, forgetful
- Being irritable, constantly in a bad mood
- Headaches, chest pain and stomach problems
- Allergic reactions (e.g. skin conditions or asthma)
- Difficulty going to sleep
- Overeating or not eating properly

Planning and managing your research 107

- New addictions or substance abuses
- Depression, constant sadness
- Being withdrawn

Please note that these are only indicators. They should not be trusted for self-diagnosis. On the other hand, you would not expect all these signs to be present in someone who was feeling stressed. If you are feeling stressed, you should **consult a professional** for a more rigorous diagnosis.

Tips on managing stress

Here are some tips about what to do to manage your stress levels:

- Try not to worry about things outside of your control. Instead, try to identify the sources of stress in your life (known as **stressors**).
- **Talk to someone** about it (such as a friend, a supervisor, or a university counsellor).
- Start a **reflective journal**: it may make it easier to write things down and reflect on how you are feeling, then start to deal with your situation.
- Reflect on how you currently cope with stress: there are healthy and unhealthy ways, so try not to start any new unhealthy habits.
- Do some regular exercise.
- Ensure that you are eating a healthy diet.
- Make time every week to relax using a technique which works best for you.

The four As of stress management

- **Accept:** When you can't change a situation, sometimes you need to just accept it for what it is.
- **Avoid:** Plan ahead to rearrange your surroundings. For example, avoid taking on more than you can handle.
- **Alter:** Changing stressful situations may allow you to evade the stress altogether. This could include managing your time better or learning to be more assertive (see Chapter 18).
- **Adapt:** By anticipating the stressors in your life and making plans to adapt, you can save yourself a lot of aggravation. This may require you to change your thinking, feelings or actions in anticipation of a perceived future event.

Source: MAYO Clinic Health System (2021)

Summary

In this chapter, we have considered some ways in which you can plan and manage your research more effectively, and how to deal with stress. Undertaking a doctoral research study is a difficult and complex task. There are bound to be highs and lows along your journey. It will require considerable time and effort for you to succeed. Planning and time management can help you to get the most out of the resources you have available. Stress management can help you to avoid becoming overburdened or unwell, or to address difficult times in your research journey with more knowledge and confidence.

References

Coaching Positive Performance (2018). *17 Essential Time Management Skills*. https://www.coachingpositiveperformance.com/17-essential-time-management-skills/

Fontana, D. (1993). *Managing Stress*. Abingdon: Routledge.

Horn, R. (2012) *Researching and Writing Dissertations: A complete guide for business and management students*. 2nd edn. London: CIPD.

Lazarus, R. and Cohen, J. (1977). *Stress, Appraisal and Coping*. New York: Springer.

Mayo Clinic Health System (2021). *The 4 A's of Stress Relief*. Available at: https://www.mayoclinichealthsystem.org/hometown-health/speaking-of-health/the-4-as-of-stress-relief

McMillan, K. and Weyers, J. (2011). *How to Write Dissertations and Project Reports*. 2nd edn. Upper Saddle River, NJ: Prentice Hall.

Rivera, J., Levine, R. and Wright, S. (2005). Completing a scholarly project during residency training: Perspectives of residents who have been successful. *Journal of General Internal Medicine*, 20(4), pp. 366–369.

18 Managing your supervisory relationships

Introduction

Your supervisory relationships are key to success in your doctoral journey. Whilst some aspects are beyond your control, there are ways you can manage your relationship with them to get the most out of them. In this chapter, we shall explore different models of the supervision process, the expectations which you should have of your supervisors and also what you need to do yourself. After this, we shall consider how best to prepare for supervisory meetings and the need to develop assertiveness.

Models of supervision

The dance metaphor

According to Derounian (2011), your supervisory relationships can be viewed like performing a **dance** together:

- The dance is your **thesis document**.
- The **content** of your writing is like dance steps.
- Like dance steps, these need to be **executed correctly** (e.g. academic writing conventions, referencing, etc.).
- Like dance choreography, there needs to be an **overall message** which comes through your thesis.
- Just as in dancing, there is a **personal relationship** between you and your supervisors which will affect the quality of the outcome.
- Finally, just as there is another intangible or "X-factor" in dancing (sometimes referred to as grace or poise), the same is true in research. You need to **develop your "voice"** as an academic researcher and writer. This will demonstrate your confidence to communicate from your research identity.

Supervisory styles

According to Gatfield (2005), supervisory approaches can be measured in terms of the level of structure and the level of support that they provide (see Figure 18.1). This leads to a model with four basic supervisory styles:

- A **pastoral** supervisor is high in support but low in structure. A pastoral supervisor emphasises caring for you as a whole person.

DOI: 10.4324/9781003434344-24

110   *After submitting your proposal*

- A **directorial** supervisor is low in support but high in structure. Directorial supervisors emphasise seeing the doctoral process as managing a sequence of interdependent tasks.
- A **contractual** supervisor is high in both structure and support. Contractual supervisors focus on their commitment to support you to achieve your doctorate and understand that this requires both nurturing and task management.
- The fourth supervisory style is called **laisser-faire** and refers to supervisors who are both low in structure and low in support. It has been written in grey text because it is viewed as being unprofessional.

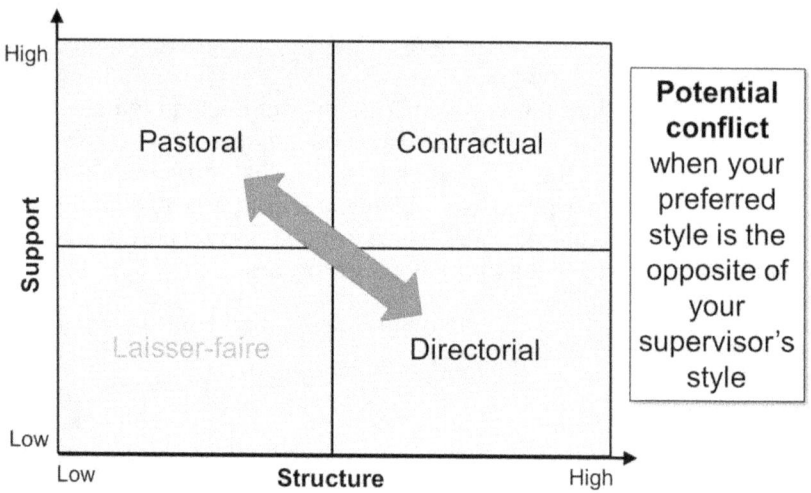

Figure 18.1 Dimensions of supervisory relationships. Adapted from Gatfield (2005: 317)

Obviously these four supervisory types are rather stereotypical, and reality will place supervisors onto more of a spectrum. However, the main point of this model is to explain that conflicts between students and supervisors can arise when a supervisor's preferred style is different from a student's preferred style. It may be that you need a certain supervisory style at a certain point in your research journey. It may also be that you have a supervisory team where the different members have complementary preferred styles. This can be to your advantage provided that your team understands which style should be used by whom and when.

Gurr's rackety bridge

According to Gurr (2001), the doctoral journal can be viewed as attempting to cross a rackety bridge (see Figure 18.2).

Doctoral students begin their journey fully dependent upon their supervisors. Their supervisors respond to their needs with appropriate support. The end goal of supervision is for doctoral students to become fully autonomous so their supervisors will try to assess how well they are developing and pull back from their hands-on approach to a more hands-off approach.

Managing your supervisory relationships 111

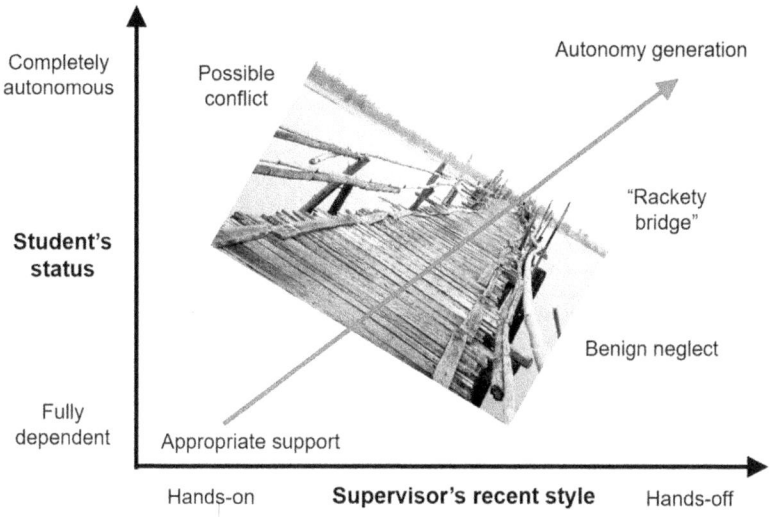

Figure 18.2 Gurr's model of student autonomy development. Adapted from Gurr (2001: 87)

The problem is the view they have of their student may not be accurate – they might need more help than their supervisors think they do, or they might need less help. This can lead to problems on either side which is the source of Gurr's metaphor as he views it like trying to cross a broken bridge with a risk of falling off on either side. If you fall off to the left, then this may lead to conflict as your supervisors are trying to help you more than you need. If you fall off to the right, then you may feel neglected because your supervisors have withdrawn their support out of the mistaken belief that you are more autonomous than you actually are. This is described as benign neglect as it is not intentional.

Having appropriate expectations

In order for your supervisory relationships to work well, it is important that you have appropriate expectations, both of your supervisors and also of what you are expected to do. We shall consider these two sides to the relationship in turn.

Supervisors

You should expect your supervisors to:

- Be available for supervisory meetings to assess your progress honestly, provide you with verbal or written feedback and to agree next steps for your research and help you set goals for your next meeting.
- Advise you about reading and research and help you to develop your idea.
- Help you to improve your research and writing ability.
- Assist you to obtain other forms of training, e.g. in research software.
- Provide you with guidance and support throughout.
- Review whether your research is manageable, suitably focused and clearly prescribed.
- Advise you on the preparation of your thesis document (in terms of its structure, content, coherence and presentation).

However, you should **not** expect your supervisors to:

- Provide you with a "ready-made" research area.
- Take responsibility for the progress of your doctoral research.
- Chase you to make an appointment with them.
- Tell you in advance whether you will ultimately succeed, even if they approve of your current level of progress.
- Respond to your emails immediately, out of hours, on annual leave or over the weekend.
- Read your work at short notice or see you without an appointment.
- Assist you with continual revisions of draft chapters.
- Proofread or edit your work.

Doctoral students

You should:

- Work conscientiously and independently, following your supervisor's guidance and feedback.
- Be **proactive** by raising problems or difficulties with your supervisors early on.
- Give your supervisors **sufficient notice** of requested meetings and send your draft work in advance.
- Prepare for supervisory meetings having addressed prior action points with a clear agenda for the meeting.
- **Take notes** during supervision meetings and send your supervisors a meeting summary soon after the meeting.
- **Take responsibility for your own progress** by regularly reviewing your personal timeline (e.g. Gantt chart) to ensure your research is on track.

Preparing for supervisions

In preparation for your supervision meetings, you should:

- Try to focus on one main subject in each meeting so that you ensure that it is covered well.
- **Organise** your paperwork before, during and after the meeting.
- **Agree on actions and dates**. This is a form of public goal setting which will improve your outcomes (see Hayes et al., 1985).
- Let go of your draft at the right moment – the best time is probably about **3 to 5 working days** before the meeting so that it is still fresh in your mind and your supervisors have sufficient time to schedule going through it.

After the meeting, if your institution does not have a formal system for recording supervision progress you should send a **supervision meeting summary sheet** to your supervisors via email within 2 to 3 days. This should include a summary of your discussion, the agreed actions by both you and them and the agreed date of the next meeting (see Figure 18.3).

Managing your supervisory relationships

Name	Student No	Date of meeting	Supervisor
Amy Fowler	111111111	2/05/24	Dr P. Samuels

Summary of meeting:

- ☐ Discussed the viability of my research idea – consumer attitudes and behaviour towards sustainable fashion brands – and its potential emphasis.
- ☐ ...

Agreed action points:

- ☐ Start collecting information and reading as much as possible from varied quality sources and, in particular, investigate academic journal articles that focus on the same subject area.
- ☐ ...

Date/time of next meeting: 24/6/24 at 10.00am

Figure 18.3 Example supervision meeting summary sheet

Learning to be assertive

Introduction

Many students fail to get what they need in supervisory relationships because they either stay quiet or don't know how to ask without appearing rude or aggressive. This is especially true of international students studying in the UK who may come from a more patriarchal culture where supervisors are highly respected.

Three approaches to others in relationship are shown in Figure 18.4.

Submissive or non-assertive people respect others, but they do not respect themselves. This means they do not get what they need. **Aggressive** people respect themselves, but they do not respect others. This means they may antagonise others and not get what they need. However, **assertive** people respect others but also respect themselves. This enables them to get what they need.

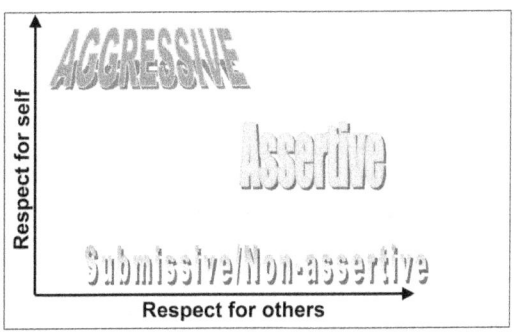

Figure 18.4 Approaches to relationships

Definition of assertiveness

Assertive people:

- Believe in respecting others and themselves, and that they have values and rights.
- Believe that they have a right to ask for what they want, have an opinion, make their own decisions, make mistakes and have their successes celebrated.
- They also believe that they can change their mind, be independent, be respected and refuse to do something they are asked, especially if they believe that it would be unhelpful to the overall success of their doctoral research project.

Source: Smith (2011)

Assertiveness techniques

According to Larsen and Jordan (2017), there are three main assertiveness techniques:

- **Broken record:** Find a suitable phrase to express yourself then repeat it without becoming emotional or justifying yourself further until you are listened to. For example, "This item is faulty. Under the sale of goods act I am entitled to my money back."
- **Empathy:** Express how you feel and that you are trying to understand how the other person feels. For example, "I understand you need help but I'm sorry I can't this time because ..."
- Offer a **compromise**. However, this should only be done whilst maintaining your self-respect.

A combination of all three techniques is often best. The skill is to know how best to combine these techniques in a particular situation.

Additional advice for successful supervisory relationships

How to nurture your supervisors

Here is some additional advice from Roberts (2010):

- Establish norms of how you will work together, such as the length and regularity of your meetings and how far in the advice you should send your draft work.
- Try to **incorporate your supervisors' recommendations into your revisions** (at least in part). Otherwise, they might become discouraged and not invest so much effort in giving you detailed feedback another time.
- Respect the time constraints of your supervisory meetings. For example, if you have agreed in advance that they are only for one hour, then do not expect to go over this time limit.
- Take the initiative, but expect guidance.
- **Maintain** *contact* – avoiding communicating with your supervisor team because you cannot face a problem is nearly always a bad strategy. You need to find the courage to be responsible and open when a problem is small rather than face negative consequences when it becomes too big.

Managing your supervisory relationships

Above all, remember, it is **your** doctorate and thesis, not theirs.
Here is some further advice from Vitae (2022):

- Keep things in perspective – you are both human, so either of you might have a bad day leading to a bad supervision meeting
- Ask for feedback – don't wait to be told what to do
- Show your enthusiasm
- Meet deadlines – set a good example

Dealing with criticism

If you receive feedback on your work which you perceive to be critical, consider the following:

- Try to take criticism of your work objectively, not personally. Try to get over your emotional reaction first then come back to it later so that you can evaluate it more objectively. Ask yourself, "are the points they made valid, and can they help me to improve my work and become a better researcher or writer?"
- Remember that your supervisors want you to succeed.
- You should also realise that having feedback is much better than not having it, even if it appears critical and negative.

If things become really difficult

If you have tried the above techniques but none of them have worked and you feel you have a problem with your supervisors, this is what you should do:

- Contact your doctoral course director (informally at first). You could begin by asking them for advice then ask them what the procedures are. This will help you to **empower yourself**, so you realise that you are not a victim and that you have choices.
- **Keep a record of all issues:** by this stage, you may be required to present factual evidence, such as email threads.
- **Seek a resolution:** there may be an existing procedure, such as a meeting between you, one or more of your supervisors, your course director and your student representative.

There are essentially four possible outcomes:

- You realise that you are to blame and change.
- Your supervisory team accepts they were at fault, and they change.
- You both realise that there is blame on both sides and you both change.
- You are unable to reach an agreement. This is the point at which trust has broken down even though you have done your best to resolve the situation, so this is when your doctoral course director should consider changing your supervisory team.

As a research project coordinator of about 1,500 students per year, I find that many students ask me for a new supervisor for trivial reasons when they have not attempted this resolution process. However, a few students genuinely reach this point and I do my best to intervene and help them.

Summary

Your supervisory relationships are very important to the overall success of your doctoral studies. Supervisors have different styles and prefer to operate in different ways, so you will need to get to know them and understand how best to manage your relationships with them. If you can present yourself as enthusiastic, reliable and organised, then you will encourage them to respond in a similar manner.

Most supervisors generally want you to succeed even if you find their advice or approach difficult at times. In order to deal with negative situations, you will need to learn to sometimes overcome your emotional reactions and focus on what you are trying to achieve in the long term. You are on a journey of discovery about your chosen research topic and also about yourself, not only as a researcher but also as a person. This may require you to learn to be more assertive at times so that you get what you need.

References

Derounian, J. (2011). Shall we dance? The importance of staff–student relationships to undergraduate dissertation preparation. *Active Learning in Higher Education*, 12(2), pp. 91–100.

Gatfield, T. (2005). An investigation into PhD supervisory management styles: Development of a dynamic conceptual model and its management. *Journal of Higher Education Policy and Management*, 27(3), pp. 311–325.

Gurr, G. (2001). Negotiating the "rackety bridge" – A dynamic model for aligning supervisory style with research student development. *Higher Education Research and Development*, 20(1), pp. 80–92.

Hayes, S. C., Rosenfarb, I., Wulfert, E., Munt, E. D., Korn, Z. and Zettle, R. D. (1985). Self-reinforcement effects: An artifact of social standard setting. *Journal of Applied Behavior Analysis*, 18(3), pp. 201–214.

Larsen, K. L. and Jordan, S. S. (2017). Assertiveness training. In: V. Zeigler-Hill and T. Shackelford, eds. *Encyclopedia of Personality and Individual Differences*. New York: Springer nature. https://doi.org/10.1007/978-3-319-28099-8_882-1

Roberts, C. (2010) *The Dissertation Journey: A practical and comprehensive guide to planning, writing and defending your dissertation*. 2nd edn. London: SAGE.

Smith, M. J. (2011) *When I Say No, I Feel Guilty*. New York: Bantam.

Vitae (2022) *Supervision and Key Relationships*. Available at: https://www.vitae.ac.uk/doing-research/doing-a-doctorate/starting-a-doctorate/supervision-and-key-relationships

19 Next steps in your research

Introduction

Once you have submitted your proposal, you are moving from the conceptual phase to the **critical phase** of your doctoral research (see Chapter 12). In this final chapter, we shall briefly explore the common tasks you will need to work on during your critical phase.

Drafting your introduction chapter

Please also refer to the section on rewriting an introduction in Chapter 16.

Your introduction chapter to your thesis should be an extension of your introduction in your proposal. Many of the principles explained in Chapters 3 and 9 can be applied to it. You will need to go into more depth in your background and problem statement, but they should follow the same principles with unique distinct paragraph topics in your background being combined together and focused in your problem statement. Again, the combination of your background and your problem statement from your rationale for choosing your research topic.

The number of objectives and research questions might increase slightly, but their style is essentially the same as for your proposal. There may be some additional sections that you need to add to this chapter, such as your potential contribution.

However, you need to remember the bear and the fish metaphor on the front cover of this book – you will not impress your examiners by providing an overly long or complex introductory chapter which does not serve its required purpose of introducing and justifying your research study. Any changes you make to your proposal introduction should therefore be carefully considered with the expectations of your main audience in mind.

Doing and drafting your full literature review

As for your thesis introduction, your full literature review chapter should be an extension of your literature review in your proposal. Again, the style will be similar to that of a proposal literature review which was explained in Chapter 10.

You may have slightly more themes. They will no doubt be longer, and they may be divided into subthemes, but you should not over-structure your review so that you leave sufficient opportunities for deeper, critical writing. You will obviously need to obtain more references and read in more depth, but the references you have already obtained and read for your proposal can form the basis for your extended literature review.

DOI: 10.4324/9781003434344-25

Your argument needs to be evidence-based and flow from one paragraph to the next. You should show critical thinking in your choice of supporting evidence and the length and style of your citations. The topics and points of your paragraphs need to be clear, and your paragraphs should be between 60 and 180 words long. You need to include theoretical perspectives and critical analysis. All these issues were discussed in Chapters 6–8 and 10.

Thesis literature reviews tend to be about 25% of the total word count. They should have a discussion at, or near, the end that is focused on your context and draws together the findings from the themes you have already presented. You might then finish your review with a conclusion in which you reappraise your research questions in the light of your findings in order to justify undertaking your research study.

Doing a full literature review is a complex task, so you may need to break it down with a work breakdown structure as explained in Chapter 17. You may also need several versions of your literature review as tasks on your Gantt chart, so it is clear when you plan to complete them and what feedback you are hoping to obtain from your supervisors.

Drafting your methodology/methods chapter

As for your first two thesis chapters, your methodology/methods chapter should also be an extension of your methodology/methods section from your proposal. It will probably be about 15–20% of your total wordcount. The main difference between the proposal and the thesis versions is the tense and style: your thesis version should be written in the **past tense** with a **more definite rationale style of argument** as the research will have been undertaken by the time this chapter is read.

As for your proposal, the methodology/methods chapter should start with an introduction and be divided into sections which follow a logical order, as explained in Chapter 12. You are also advised to **include a conceptual framework** (see Chapter 11) as they are very helpful and there should be sufficient wordcount for this. However, you should be careful not to explain things to the reader that they already know, or add more sections which overlap in content and make the overall rationale and plan for carrying out your research project less clear.

Nevertheless, there may be sufficient wordcount for more discussion towards the end of some of your sections. This could address issues such as your choices compared with viable alternatives, how these choices have been implemented and potential limitations or issues you may face when carrying out the research. If you are carrying out quantitative analysis, you may have a longer discussion about validity, reliability and your hypotheses for statistical analysis. Again, please refer to Chapter 12 for an initial explanation.

Like the introduction, there is no need for a conclusion at the end of this chapter.

Requesting ethics approval

Before you carry out primary data collection, most institutions require you to have first obtained ethics approval, so this will need to be completed during your critical phase. It is important to understand and appreciate the principles of ethical conduct in research. These relate to **protecting your research participants** and the **data** they provide and carrying out your research in an **ethical manner**. Please refer to the *Ethics* section of Chapter 12 and Oliver (2010).

Ethics approval works like an **insurance policy**: in the unlikely event that something goes wrong during your research and you have ethics approval then your institution is responsible; **if you do not have ethics approval, then you are personally liable**.

The elements of the ethics approval process will be specific to your institution, and you should receive advice and training on this. For general information on the ethics process, please refer to https://www.ukri.org/councils/esrc/guidance-for-applicants/research-ethics-guidance/.

Designing your data collection instrument

The final task we shall consider during the critical phase of your doctorate is the design of a data collection instrument if you are undertaking primary data collection. Your design should be based on your research questions and objectives (see Chapter 3), and your conceptual framework (see Chapter 11).

If you are undertaking a survey, you need to think carefully about what questions you wish to include here so that you can obtain the most useful data to answer your research questions and achieve your objectives. You should avoid asking complicated questions. For questionnaires, data analysis is often based on a research design which involves a combination of answers to different questions.

Your supervisors should give you feedback on your draft data collection instrument. You can also show some of your fellow students a draft version to see whether it makes sense to them. This might also help you to think about an example data set for your data analysis. However, you should not undertake any actual data collection until your ethics request has been approved.

For more information, please refer to the books in the bibliography list below.

Summary

In this final chapter, we have looked forward to your doctoral journey from the completion of your proposal to the next phase, known as the critical phase. Much of the work you have undertaken in creating your proposal can be reused here, and many of the principles we have already covered in creating sections of your proposal can be applied to the first three chapters of a standard doctoral thesis, namely the introduction, literature review and the methodology or method chapters. This chapter has provided some more detail into this process and includes some initial advice on ethics and data collection instrument design.

I wish you every success with your doctoral studies! I hope you have found my book useful.

Bibliography

Alvesson, M. (2013). *Constructing Research Questions: Doing interesting research*. London: SAGE.
Fink, A. (2009). *How to Conduct Surveys: A step-by-step guide*. 4th edn. London: SAGE.
Frazer, L. and Lawley, M. (2000). *Questionnaire Design and Administration: A practical guide*. Chichester: Wiley.

Hammersley, M. and Atkinson, P. (1995). *Ethnography: Principles in practice*. 3rd edn. London: Routledge.
Oliver, P. (2010). *The Student's Guide to Research Ethics*. 2nd edn. Maidenhead: Open University Press.
Oppenheim, A. N. (2005). *Questionnaire Design, Interviewing and Attitude Measurement*.New edn. London: Pinter.
Rea, L. M. and Parker, R. A. (2005). *Designing and Conducting Survey Research: A comprehensive guide*. 4th edn. San Francisco: Wiley.
Rubin, H. and Rubin, I. (2004). *Qualitative Interviewing: The art of hearing data*. 2nd edn. London: SAGE.

Index

50-40-10 principle 56

abduction *see* approach, abductive
academic writing 5, 21; clarity 27, 30, 95; functional skills 5; hedging 31, 59; passive voice 27, 55, 75; simplicity 27, 96; tense 28, 118
academic writing style 27; acronyms 29; apostrophes 28; contractions 28; emotive language 30; Latin abbreviations 29; personal language 27
academic writing tree 5
acronyms *see* academic writing style, acronyms
AI *see* artificial intelligence
aim 18
aim evaluation 18
aim writing 18
annotated bibliography *see* literature review, annotated bibliography
apostrophes *see* academic writing style, apostrophes
approach 69; abductive 69; deductive 69; inductive 69
argument 3, 23, 27, 30, 38, 41
argument planning 43
argument style 41, 50, 67, 72; adversarial 41, 50, 72; single argument/opinion 41; discursive 41–42, 59
artificial intelligence 14, 34
assertiveness 106, 114; definition 114; techniques 114
audience 45, 66, 96
autonomy generation 111

background 49
bear eating fish 11

career goals *see* topic selection strategy, career goals
case study *see* strategy, case study
charts *see* quantitative analysis, charts
ChatGPT 14, 34
citation rate 12

citing: direct 86; indirect 86; *see* referencing, citing
claims 32
concept map 57
conceptual framework 61, 63, 68, 72, 118
conclusion *see* literature review, conclusion
conflict resolution 115
contingency planning 77, 82, 105
contractions *see* academic writing style, contractions
convergent thinking 11
creativity *see* topic selection, creativity
critical analysis 59, 118
critical analysis, depth of questions 60
critical realism *see* philosophy, critical realism
critical thinking 8, 34, 38, 56, 59, 75, 103, 118
criticism 115

dance metaphor 109
data analysis 67, 74; qualitative 73–75; quantitative 74; mixed methods 74
data collection 72; focus groups 70; interviews 70; observations 72; primary 4, 63, 72, 96, 118; questionnaires 70; reliability 73; secondary 4, 71, 73; validity 73
data collection instrument 63, 72, 82, 119
data types 74
databases *see* literature searching, databases
DECJAD 78
deduction *see* approach, inductive
descriptive analysis *see* quantitative analysis, descriptive
discursive style argument *see* argument style, discursive
discursive style paragraph *see* paragraph, discursive style
dissertation *see* thesis
divergent thinking 11
doctoral research benefits 4, 8

emotive language *see* academic writing style, emotive language
empathy 114

empirical literature 56, 58
ethics 76, 82, 105, 118
evidence 30, 33, 38, 40–41, 53, 55, 59, 78, 86, 115, 118

feedback *see* proposal feedback
figures 55, 88
finishing energy 15, 105
focus 41, 51, 71, 74, 78, 96, 99–100, 102, 104, 112, 114
focus groups *see* data collection, focus groups
Four As of stress management 107
front matter 15, 53, 54, 96, 100
functional skills *see* academic writing, functional skills

Gantt charts 81, 98, 112, 118
genre 5, 16, 53, 97, 101
getting started 105
Google 88, 90
Google Scholar 12, 55, 89
grammar *see* academic writing, grammar
Grammarly 34
grounded theory *see* qualitative analysis, grounded theory
Gurr's rackety bridge 110–111

hedging *see* academic writing, hedging
Horn, R. 14, 105
hypotheses 4, 51, 63, 73, 118

illumination *see* topic selection creativity, illumination
impact 24, 31, 51, 102
incubation *see* topic selection creativity, incubation
interpretivism *see* philosophy, interpretivism
interviews *see* data collection, interviews
introduction 49, 102, 117

journals *see* literature searching, electronic journals
justification 24, 51, 78, 83, 101

Latin abbreviations *see* academic writing style, Latin abbreviations
limitations 24, 51, 67, 77, 102, 118
literature review 54, 100, 117; annotated bibliography 54, 56; conclusion 61; including theory 58; narrative 4, 54; scope 55–57; systematic 4, 71; thematic 54, 61, 98
literature searching 13, 55; databases 12, 55; electronic journals 55; search engine 12, 55

method 3, 23, 66, 72, 118; data analysis 74; data collection 72
methodology 66, 118; approach 69; philosophy 68; strategy 70

Miller, G. A. 23, 96
mistakes 29, 56, 77, 95, 114
mixed methods 4, 67, 69, 74
motivation 15, 104

narrative literature review *see* literature review, narrative
non-specialist audience 19, 29, 85, 97
numerical data 74

objectives 16, 18, 23, 117
objectives evaluation 18
objectives writing 18
observations *see* data collection, observations
outline 44, 51, 102

paragraph 37; coherence 37; definition 37; discursive style 42, 59–60; length 37; point 37, 43, 45; structure 37; topic 37
passive voice 27, 55
perfectionism 105
personal language *see* academic writing style, personal language
philosophy 68, 78; critical realism 68; interpretivism 68; positivism 68; postmodernism 68; pragmatism 68
plagiarism 34
plan 3, 23, 55, 67, 78, 84, 95, 100, 107
planning 43, 81, 103
planning: contingency 77, 82, 105; dependencies 82
Poincaré, H. 11
population 70, 76–77
positivism *see* philosophy, positivism
postmodernism *see* philosophy, postmodernism
pragmatism *see* philosophy, pragmatism
presentation *see* proposal presentation
presentation delivery 98
presentation format 95
presentation principles 96
presentation questions 99
presentation structure 97
presentation technique *see* argument planning
primary analysis 75
primary data 4, 63, 72
primary research thesis 4
problem solving *see* topic selection strategy, problem solving
problem statement 23, 49, 50, 96, 102
proposal 3
proposal feedback 100, 105, 111, 115, 118
proposal presentation 95
protocol *see* method
purpose 3
purposive sampling *see* sampling, purposive

qualitative analysis 74; categories 75; grounded theory 76; primary 75; themes 75; theory generation 76
qualitative content analysis 75
quality 6, 15, 30, 62, 101, 109
quantitative analysis 74; charts 74; descriptive 74; statistical testing 74; summary statistics 74; tables 74
questionnaire: closed questions 70; open questions 71; see data collection, questionnaires
questions: deep 42, 58, 60; shallow 60
QuillBot 34
quoting 34

random sampling see sampling, random
rationale 3, 24, 41, 49, 51, 61, 67, 95, 101
reader psychology xi, 102
referencing 86; alphabetical 86; citing 33, 86; reference list 89
relevance see topic evaluation, relevance
reliability see data collection, reliability
research: mixed methods 4, 74; qualitative 4, 68–69; quantitative 4, 63, 68–69
research community 7
research design 67, 77, 119
research phase 7, 81; conceptual 7, 81; critical 7, 81, 117
research question evaluation 19
research question writing 19
research questions 16, 19, 23, 55, 61, 117
ResearchGate 12
response rate 71, 77
rewriting 35, 101

sample size 70, 98
sampling 70; non-random 70; random 70
San serif font 96
Saunders, M. N. 66–69, 75, 78
Schedule 81
scope see topic evaluation, scope
search engines see literature searching, search engines
secondary data 4, 71, 73
secondary data thesis 4
section numbering 24
sections 23
significance 7, 31, 51, 102
single argument/opinion see argument style, single argument/opinion
statistical testing see quantitative analysis, statistical testing
statistics see quantitative analysis, summary statistics
strategy 70; action research 71; case study 71; ethnography 71; experiment 71; grounded theory 71; secondary data 71; survey 71

stress 106–107; causes 106; definition 106; signs 106–107
stress management 107
structure 23; two level 23
student expectations 111–112
subjective writing 30–31
summarising 35, 61
summary statistics see quantitative analysis, summary statistics
supervision meetings 112
supervision models 109
supervisor relationship 109; handling criticism 115; difficulties 115; expectations 111
supervisory styles 109–110
survey 70, 77, 119; focus groups 70; interviews 70; questionnaire 70
systematic literature review see literature review, systematic

tables 55, 74, 88
task ranking 103
tasks 81–83, 103
tense see academic writing, tense
textual data 4, 71, 74, 76, 96
thematic literature review see literature review, thematic
theoretical framework 58, 63
theory generation see qualitative analysis, theory generation
thesis statement 51
thesis types 4
third person 27
time management 103
title writing 16
topic evaluation 14–15; interest 4, 15, 50, 55; originality 3, 15, 50; relevance 7, 50; scope 11, 13, 17, 50–51, 100; viability 3, 11, 100
topic modification 15, 100
topic selection creativity 11–13; illumination 13; incubation 13; preparation 11–13; verification 14–15
topic selection strategy 14; career goals 14; data 13–14; problem solving 14; tutor driven 14
transitional words and phrases 38–40, 43, 60
Turnitin 34

validity see data collection, validity
visual stress 96

What 3 Words 49
work breakdown structure 104–105, 118
writing numbers 30
writing process 43
writing style see academic writing style

For Product Safety Concerns and Information please contact our EU
representative GPSR@taylorandfrancis.com
Taylor & Francis Verlag GmbH, Kaufingerstraße 24, 80331 München, Germany

www.ingramcontent.com/pod-product-compliance
Lightning Source LLC
Chambersburg PA
CBHW080613230426
43664CB00019B/2880